"*Called to Serve* speaks from experience and offers hope like no other book geared toward military families. Picking it up might be the first step to healing. A must read."

—Karen Kingsbury, *New York Times* best-selling
author of *Unlocked* and *Shades of Blue*

"*Called to Serve* is a must read for anyone involved with military life and families. The Monettis discuss the full range of topics and issues that confront today's active duty, guard, and reserve families, from routine inconveniences to life-impacting tragedies to intimate relationships. Regardless of whether the service member is a veteran of numerous deployments or fresh out of basic training, an officer or enlisted, the Monettis' book is the go-to reference for successfully journeying through a life of defending America. I heartily encourage the reading of *Called to Serve!*"

—Jonathan George, Brigadier General (Ret.),
Former Director of Strategic Capabilities Policy, National Security
Council and Executive Office of the President, Washington, DC

"I was so captivated by Tony and Penny's candid marital stories I couldn't put the book down. Their straightforward way of sharing personal trials and successes had me both laughing and in tears. They have highlighted hidden areas the enemy has targeted to destroy military marriages, and they courageously share how they were able to shut down the enemy's arsenal and turn their situations into victory! *Called to Serve* is a must read for all married couples and for intercessors. As a praying woman, I now feel better equipped to pray for our men and women in the military. Thank you, Tony and Penny!"

—Sharon Stark Niedzinski, author of *Heaven Has Blue Carpet*

"Through poignant, humorous, and heartfelt personal accounts, Tony and Penny Monetti encourage, equip, and inspire military families for the challenges faced by those 'called to serve.' This mission-enhancing weapon should be a part of every marriage's arsenal."

—US Congresswoman Vicky Hartzler, Missouri, 4th District

"Tony and Penny Monetti have provided military families with a great resource in *Called to Serve*. As a former military chaplain, I know the strain military families are under with constant deployments and long separations. This results in affairs, abuse, distrust, alienation, and divorce. (The divorce rate in the military is four times that of the civilian world.) This is not just a devotional book, it's a book on lessons learned from a couple who have been in the military for over twenty years. I would hope that every couple in the military would get a copy of this book and study it together."

—Chaplain (Major) Den Slattery (Ret.)

"The Monettis have been 'called to serve' twice in life, first as a military family on active duty and now for their book for other military families. They have very beautifully and thoughtfully woven together vignettes and lessons from their lives to help other families navigating the always challenging paths of military life. The spiritual underpinnings of their book are constant, strong, and uplifting throughout."

—The Honorable Allen Clark, author of *Wounded Soldier, Healing Warrior* and founder of Combat Faith Lay Ministry

CALLED TO SERVE

Encouragement, Support, and Inspiration
for Military Families

Lt. Col. Tony Monetti & Penny Monetti

Discovery House.
from Our Daily Bread Ministries

Called to Serve: Encouragement, Support, and Inspiration for Military Families
© 2011 by Tony Monetti and Penny Monetti
All rights reserved.

Discovery House is affiliated with Our Daily Bread Ministries, Grand Rapids, Michigan.

Requests for permission to quote from this book should be directed to: Permissions Department, Discovery House, P.O. Box 3566, Grand Rapids, MI 49501, or contact us by e-mail at permissionsdept@dhp.org

Interior design by Melissa Elenbaas

Library of Congress Cataloging-in-Publication Data

Monetti, Tony.
Called to serve : encouragement, support, and inspiration for military families / Tony Monetti & Penny Monetti.

   p. cm.
   Includes bibliographical references.
   ISBN 978-1-57293-458-0
   1. Families of military personnel—United States. 2. United States—Armed Forces—Military life.   3. United States—Armed Forces—Religious life.   4. Families of military personnel—Religious life—United States. 5. Christian life—United States. 6. Sociology, Military—United States. 7. Monetti, Tony. 8. Monetti, Penny. 9. Families of military personnel—United States—Biography.   10. United States. Air Force—Officers—Biography. I. Monetti, Penny. II. Title.
UB403.M66 2011
355.1'20973—dc22

                                                                                              2011001286

Printed in the United States of America

Fifth printing in 2015

Contents

• PART 1 •

Fear

• PART 2 •

Transition

• PART 3 •

Loneliness and Grief

Preface

It is God who arms me with strength and makes my way perfect. He makes my feet like the feet of a deer; he enables me to stand on the heights. He trains my hands for battle.
Psalm 18:32–34

Whether you serve on the home front, defend our great country on the battlefront, or are a loving military family member or supportive friend, get ready to experience God's strength to meet your daily needs.

Our formation has experienced God's strength. In military terms, a formation is when two or more aircraft fly in close proximity to provide mutual support. We have flown in formation as a military family for more than twenty-three years and have logged many adventurous flights. We have also suffered severe turbulence and nearly crashed, but were saved by the guidance of professional mentors, fellow warriors and spouses, and God.

We have poured our military experience into the book you now hold in your hands. Our goal is to strengthen, encourage, and equip Armed Forces families and those who love them for the extraordinary challenges that the warrior's lifestyle presents by providing life lessons from our military years that we have lived and loved.

The warrior's lifestyle has presented unique challenges in our lives. We know how to pack bed hardware in Alabama so that when the shipment arrives in a foreign country, we won't be camping on the floor. We know the heartache of pulling our children from one school and enrolling them in another, sometimes three times in one year, moving them away from friends, and then reassuring them that they will make new ones—yet again. We have felt the gut-wrenching emptiness having to say or hear, "I'm leaving tomorrow. I can't tell you where I'm going or how long I will be gone. It may be six months or possibly a year." We know about midnight goodbyes with a child clinging to his mother as his daddy taxis down the tarmac, wondering if he will ever return. We know the euphoria of welcoming a deployed warrior back home, and then the frustration of figuring out how to piece back together the formerly separated family. We've experienced the fear of combat against an unknown enemy. We have hurdled the destructive temptations of alcohol, depression, and pornography. Like you, we know military life's challenges.

Through riveting, heartwarming, and humorous stories, we expose the challenges and temptations that every warrior and spouse face during their military career from the vantage points of both the "warrior" and the "spouse." It is our goal to not only offer hope, but also provide informational weapons to smoke out and combat the top stressors affecting today's military family.

Select professional Christian counselors and Armed Forces chaplains from various denominations identified the top stressors waging war within military families. Their expert wisdom appears in several chapters. Five categories—Fear, Transition, Loneliness and Grief, Destructive Behaviors, and Communication—are tackled and paired with related Scripture. A heartfelt prayer and several thought-provoking questions follow each chapter, perfect for individual reflection, a couple's study, or small group discussions. Issue-related links are also provided in the chapters and at the book's end. Family and friends nudged to help the military but unsure where to focus their energies will find numerous patriotic organizations listed for reference. Now, good intentions can be launched into action.

When you turn the last page of *Called to Serve*, you are not left stranded. Visit our website, Pennymonetti.com, and click "Called to Serve Ministries" for upcoming events, updated military support links to websites, and related blogs. Visit the support page where military warriors, spouses, and patriotic Americans can offer and receive encouragement, confidentially share challenges, and swap stories with fellow military members. A prayer request page offers a refuge for military families to connect and prayerfully support each other.

We thank you from the bottom of our hearts for serving America in whatever capacity you have chosen and for answering your "Call to Serve," and we welcome you into our formation.

Only through Him,

Lt. Col. Tony and Penny Monetti

Acknowledgments

We offer our deepest gratitude to the men and women who set their boots on foreign soil, leaving their comfortable homes and loving families to selflessly defend America's freedom.

To the spouses who independently manage households, sell homes, uproot children, repeatedly leave friendships, and miraculously transform each new place into a loving home.

To the courageous parents who protected their children from stepping into oncoming traffic, playing with matches, and wading into the pool's deep end and who now surrender those same children to God's loving care while their children heed the military's call.

To every American who proudly wears red, white, and blue on days other than the Fourth of July, who sheds a tear while the national anthem plays, and who faithfully prays for troops they have never met.

And finally, to those family members of fallen soldiers who rendered the ultimate sacrifice—their very lives. A few words of thanks do not suffice, so we dedicate this entire book to you with immeasurable gratitude.

To God be the glory: For His hand's guidance as we typed our chapters and sought expert counsel on tough issues. For His protection while we strove to declare His truths. For His embracing love, and for being a fortress of strength for those serving our country on the battlefront as well as on the home front. For His availability, guidance, and saving grace for all those who ask.

To our loving families who prayed not only for this book's completion but for the lives it will touch. To Angela Dearduff for her constant encouragement and editing help. To the dynamic publishing team at Discovery House for making this experience possible, with special thanks to our wonderful editor, Miranda Gardner. To our counseling team members, who wove their wisdom throughout the book to guide a people and a country they hold dear: Stephen F. Pringle, M.A., D.Min., LPC, and Cheryl Mark, M.A., LPC, from Diakonos Christian Counseling; Chaplain (LTC) Phillip Pringle, US Army; Dr. Daniel Roysden, US Navy Chaplain (Ret.); Chaplain Major R. Martin Fitzgerald, US Air Force; Lindy Williamson, MSW, International Critical Incident Stress Foundation instructor and National Veterans Foundation consultant; Marshele Carter Waddell, inspirational speaker, author, and post-traumatic stress disorder expert; and Jenny Andrews, programs manager and post-traumatic stress disorder counseling supervisor at notalone.com.

We also would like to thank MSgt. Shane Lacaillade, US Air Force Independent Duty Medical Technician, Cheryl Dodson, Ursula Martin, Cynthia Culver, the Chick TDY "peeps," Josh Pfaff, those who contributed anonymously, and all the worthy organizations listed in the back of this book that honor and support military men and women through their selfless volunteer efforts while our military members uphold America's freedom—we salute you.

PART 1

Fear

ONE

God's Got My Twelve

Learning to Trust God

The Lord is near. Do not be anxious about anything, but in everything, by prayer and petition, with thanksgiving, present your requests to God. And the peace of God, which transcends all understanding, will guard your hearts and your minds in Christ Jesus.

Philippians 4:5–7

The bus's icy wipers fought to cling to the frozen windshield. Twelve anxious spouses from the 668th B-52 Bomb Squadron, stationed in Rome, New York, loaded their coat-covered, pajama-clad, sleepy-eyed toddlers and young children onto the navy blue bus. The engine's loud revving pierced the eerie midnight silence. The bus's tires furrowed fresh tracks on the snow-covered road that bordered the gloomy Air Force runway. The squadron commander had arranged a rare opportunity for spouses and children to bid their warriors goodbye, possibly for the last time, before they departed for a brewing war.

We pulled onto the tarmac where a massive green KC-135 refueling plane created the backdrop for a bustle of military activity. My then two-year-old son suddenly burst out from his drowsiness, "That Daddy, Mommy! Daddy fly his co-plane!" Nico pointed to the sea of flight suits and leather bomber jackets. Any soldier wearing the olive-green uniform was dubbed *daddy*. Crew members cracked many a joke when Nico mistook one of them for his father. The runway floodlights illuminated an assembly line of *daddies* passing their flight bags down the line, up a metal stairway, and into the plane's belly like a well-conducted symphony. I thought, *Can't you guys load slower?* The deployment happened so quickly.

Only two days earlier my husband, Tony, received open-ended orders to a location he could not share with me. His deployment would last six months to a year—time would tell. Tony started preparing me for this day three years ago, before we married. Serving in combat is the reality of joining the military, but every warrior and military family hopes that conflict will never happen. However, war in Iraq knocked at our country's door, and the US military hastily answered.

The countdown to his departure prompted trips to obtain life insurance, create a will, and grant power of attorney—just in case. Tony had promised Nico a campout when the weather warmed. Even though the fire hydrants lay buried under the January snow, Tony bought an orange, four-man tent to fulfill his promise. He transformed our living room into a campsite complete with s'mores, flashlights, and popcorn. I held back tears as my son excitedly rolled his Teenage Mutant Ninja Turtles sleeping bag next to his father's not-so-exciting blue sack. Later when Nico danced and sang his mixed-up rendition of "Jingle Bells," our laughter mingled with tears. Our unspoken words blasted the same thought: *Will this be the last time?*

Tony's crew finished loading the bags as the dreaded moment neared. *Did he have to walk toward us so fast? Slow down!* Nico leaped up into his daddy's arms. Tony and I clung to each other tightly, sandwiching Nico in an embrace. I can't remember the words spoken, just that I didn't want to let go of the man who was the crux of my existence and the heartbeat of our family. The commander's orders to board ended our goodbye. As the crew of *daddies* filtered onto the plane, our small group of spouses hugged our children closer. Hoping he could still see us standing alongside the runway, Nico and I waved at the tanker that taxied both Tony and me into unknown territory.

Along with my first deployment goodbye, I was introduced to the military spouse's troublesome trio: fear, uncertainty, and worry. If military spouses and family members leave these emotions unattended, they will become the unwanted houseguests that never leave. Yet, we greet these mental home wreckers at our mind's door, offer them our favorite recliner, and entertain them until we are mentally, physically, and spiritually drained. They startle us from a good dream, race our heartbeat, and steal away valuable rest so we become short-tempered with our family and coworkers.

The tormenting trio of emotions is destructive. I glued myself to the news channels, which broadcasted new fears continually.

Footage of allied planes blasting Iraq with bombs played on every station. I watched carefully to see if I recognized any B–52s in the mix. Televised images of a battered, bloody American taken prisoner by Iraqi soldiers saturated the news and haunted my dreams. Would I see my husband's face simulcast on every station like this poor man? My heart poured out sympathy for him and his family. I wondered whether I could handle their situation. Within weeks dishes stacked up, laundry towered, and sleep rarely visited my bed. The ulcers lining my gums caused by worry inflicted so much pain that I struggled to eat solid food and sought medical help.

Military friends invited me regularly to a Friday evening Bible study. Each time I politely excused myself thinking, *Who holds Bible studies on Friday nights?* Although I had accepted Christ as my Savior three years earlier, praying with others in someone's living room was as far out of my comfort zone as my annual PAP smear. I was raised to believe faith was a private issue, not something you shared with others, and certainly not with a group. However, one night a study member caught me off-guard and, once again, invited me. I agreed to attend. During the meeting, as individuals presented their worry-related prayer requests, a strange wave of comfort rushed over me. I wasn't alone. We all faced the same anxiety. I detected in them a peace I craved, and I prayed for the first time that God would grant me that peace. I soon realized that although I believed in a powerful God, I didn't trust Him with my daily worries or ask guidance for decisions Tony normally handled. Through studying the Bible and praying with fellow Christians, I learned that no concern was too small for God. Bible

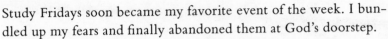

Study Fridays soon became my favorite event of the week. I bundled up my fears and finally abandoned them at God's doorstep.

From that day forth, instead of entertaining fear, I focused on maintaining my physical health, praying away my anxiety, and planning fun activities to give our spouses' worry-filled minds a reality break. Lack of sleep had invited anxiety to inhabit my mind. I began to rest when my son napped. I exercised unwanted stress away. When pesky worries tried to pitch camp in my thoughts, prayer booted them out. I attended the Friday Bible study regularly. During the week, I organized mom and kid dates, progressive dinners, and enjoyable outings. A lingerie party for wives became a big hit.

A common military saying that refers to shielding a comrade from harm stems from the numbers on a clock's face. The twelve represents what lies in front of you and the six signifies what lurks behind. When someone has "got your six," that means he or she will ward off enemies from behind.

Trusting God offered no guarantee that my husband would come home safely or that life would return to "normal," but I learned that I didn't walk alone. God cared about my daily challenges. He not only has my six; He knows what's ahead. God's got my twelve, as well.

Lord, thank you for assuring me that I am not alone. You are always near. Help me to cast anxiety at your doorstep and leave it there. When life gets hectic and uninvited worries start to invade, help my family and me experience the peace that comes only through trusting you.

WHAT WORRIES YOU? What steps are you taking to halt anxiety from holding your thoughts hostage? What activities are you participating in to help your physical, spiritual, and emotional condition? Have you invited God to walk beside you?

Resources

Combat Faith and Military Ministry encourage and strengthen Christians' faith in Jesus Christ. Learn more about these websites in the Resources section in the back of this book.

• TWO •

Fear Not

Going into Battle

Fear not, for I am with you.

Isaiah 41:10 (NKJV)

In 1991, the Department of Defense asked thousands of soldiers, airmen, and marines to defend America through Operation Desert Storm. Iraq had attacked Kuwait, and our coalition force was tasked with the responsibility of liberating Kuwait. I was a first lieutenant in the Air Force, and the time had come for me to fly my first combat mission as a B-52 pilot. Training was over—I was about to find out if I had the "right stuff." My crew deployed to the island of Diego Garcia in the Indian Ocean.

When a serviceman experiences combat for the first time, the event feels surreal. There is a powerful fear of the unknown. The military can prepare soldiers for the conflict by providing training, but soldiers need to have the one ingredient that no one can provide—courage. They must find courage within themselves. Showing up and entering the arena of war takes inner strength, and sometimes you don't know if you have that strength before the actual conflict takes place.

My first combat mission pushed me to come to grips with many aspects of my life, especially the fear of death. Prior to my mission, I wrote letters to family members in case I did not make it home. The thought of dying terrified me. Watching live media reports perpetuated that fear as the Iraqi propaganda machine televised an injured US Naval aviator prisoner of war. The bruised aviator was obviously coerced into making negative comments about America, which infuriated me. His defeated image permeated my mind.

My bomber crew, known as E-13, received orders to destroy vital targets deep in enemy territory. Within twenty-four hours, my crew would engage in combat. Flying a B-52 bomber just four hundred feet above the ground at night is inherently dangerous, but doing so against a well-equipped enemy defending its homeland increased the risk exponentially. Thoughts raced through my mind. Why was I here? Was this war worth my life? If I died, what would be next? My room began to resemble a prison cell, and I decided a change of scenery was required. As I walked along the tranquil shores of Diego Garcia, my worries turned into prayers to God for help. As always, He responded!

In the distance, I spotted a small church surrounded by palm trees. As I entered the simple white cinderblock building, a priest welcomed me in. We made small talk and shared stories about our families. Soon my anxieties began spewing out like water from a cracked dam. I explained that the following day, I would be in combat, and before I knew it I began confessing my sins and expressing my doubts. He listened intently and prayed with me, standing with one hand in the air and one on my head while I bowed down on my knees. Then I distinctly remember him saying, "God will never abandon you." Upon hearing those powerful words, I was set free from the bondage of fear like a bird from a cage. An inner strength reemerged within me. I was reassured that God *is* with me, and with God, all things are possible (see Matthew 19:26).

Most American servicemen are ready professionally for combat because our nation gives us the best training and equipment in the world. However, actually fighting an enemy that wants to kill you is unlike any training exercise. The best time to prepare for combat is now. Whether you are active duty, reserve, or a guardsman, you never know when you will be called to serve our nation in war. What works for me is striving for physical, mental, and spiritual balance.

Being in the proper physical shape provides body strength and improves self-discipline. Maintaining a healthy diet helps fuel the body properly. Each military branch has nutritional experts, fitness programs, and even contests to get your body in shape. If you're not in shape, then start an exercise program and stay committed to it. When you go to war, you never know when you will need endurance and strength. I know of warriors who were behind enemy lines and needed their bodies to survive dire situations with little to no food. Being physically fit and maintaining a healthy weight before combat is a prerequisite.

A strong body is aided by mental toughness. The enemy wants to mess with your mind. Do not allow it. You and you alone control your mind and what goes into it. During Desert Storm, the Iraqi leadership did their best to scare American warriors by showing injured prisoners of war. That fear can rip you apart and weaken your mind. I let my imagination run wild and allowed fear to grip me. But now that I have experienced that fear and conquered it, I became mentally stronger. Mental toughness and focusing your mind toward positive rather than negative, from fear to hope, will help you overcome adversity (see Jeremiah 17:7–8). Mental discipline will help you choose to fight the enemy rather than hide. You have to believe in yourself and something more. The area in my life that was most out of balance prior to my first combat mission was my personal faith.

When I asked for assistance in this area, a priest reached out and helped restore my faith. Expressing my anxieties to someone helped me realize that the root cause of my fear was doubt about my faith. I was frightened beyond belief because I was not at peace with God and knew that my life on this planet may be over tomorrow. Years earlier, I had accepted Christ as my Lord and Savior; I wholeheartedly believed in the message of salvation and was baptized. But prior to my first combat mission, I doubted my salvation. I wondered how God could love me and accept me into heaven if I had not lived my life as a Christian every day, for I was not carrying my cross daily.

It is one thing to say that you will be saved by just believing, but if you are not at peace with God, then you question your faith. At least I did. I was afraid of what awaited me on the other side should I die the next day, until that blessed man reached out and reminded me that I was not alone. All I needed to do was humble myself, pray for forgiveness, and believe that God is merciful and that His grace is sufficient for me.

The threat of combat forces you to deal with overcoming a fear of the unknown. I needed to meet with that priest to help set my mind straight and muster the courage to fight. War came quickly in my career, as I was only a new lieutenant. However, being secure in faith gave me the edge I needed to succeed. One of my favorite Bible verses is 2 Timothy 1:7: "For God did not give us a spirit of timidity, but a spirit of power, of love and of self-discipline." By maintaining proper physical, mental, and spiritual balance, I was able to stand firm and fight the enemy.

That day in the church, after confessing my sins and acknowledging to almighty God that I needed Him, helped restored peace with God. His forgiveness set me free from the fear of death and the unknown. By accepting Jesus as the Son of God and my Savior, He provided me with all that I will ever need. I hated feeling fear, but I am glad that I experienced it, because it restored my faith and made me stronger.

Being afraid before going to war is normal. How you deal with that fear will define you as a person. Turn and hide, or face the enemy and fight. For those who trust Jesus as their Savior, their survival and victory are assured, if not in this life, then in the next. No matter what would happen the following day, I was ready, for I knew that God was with me.

Thank you, Lord, for being with me and not abandoning me during my times of struggle. Give me the courage to fight when required and not to fear the unknown.

HAVE YOU EXPERIENCED COMBAT YET? Are you ready? Are you secure in your faith? List how you are maintaining a healthy balance physically, mentally, and spiritually. Have you accepted Jesus Christ as your Savior?

Resources

Combat Faith and Military Ministry encourage and strengthen Christians' faith in Jesus Christ. Learn more about these websites in the Resources section in the back of this book.

THREE

Bed Rest and Casseroles

Coping with the Unknown

The Lord himself goes before you and will be with you; he will never leave you nor forsake you. Do not be afraid; do not be discouraged.

Deuteronomy 31:8

"I'm very sorry, but you are not going anywhere for at least four weeks—total bed rest!" the military obstetrician adamantly instructed. "You have placenta previa, a condition where the organ that nourishes the baby, the placenta, partially or fully covers the cervix, the opening in which the baby exits the womb. Your cervix is completely covered," he explained.

"What about riding in a plane? I won't walk. I'll use a wheelchair," I offered. Our family was lucky to obtain a house at our new base. Getting on base usually requires a wait of six to twelve months. I added in my best pleading voice, "If we stay here, we may lose the house." The doctor sternly retorted, "If you do not remain on *strict* bed rest, at best your baby may be born premature and the organs may not be fully formed. Worst case is that you risk hemorrhaging, which could be fatal to both you and your baby."

The resolute doctor had me at placenta previa. He didn't have to convince me of the seriousness of this pregnancy's complication. As a nurse, I understood the risks of this pregnancy complication. However, the staunch doctor gave no prescription for finding temporary living arrangements for a month. He offered no guarantee for the security of Tony's dream job—flying the B1-bomber. He offered no solutions to secure a home for us in case Tony was permitted to keep his flying slot at the new base in Wichita, Kansas. He did not wave his doctor's wand and materialize an activity coordinator for my rambunctious toddler, who would soon be cooped up for a month in a tiny hotel room. (Bed rest with an eighteen-month-old toddler? Yeah, right! He obviously had no kids.) Regardless, the doctor's orders were clear: "Don't move. Don't travel. Don't get out of bed except to go to the bathroom." When Tony and I returned to Griffiss Air Force Base (AFB) in Rome, New York, to "out-process," we had no idea what process awaited us during this third military relocation.

Every military family endures the infamous "out-processing" experience countless times. Out-processing is a paperwork obstacle course that must be scaled, tunneled through, and hurdled over in order to exit one base so a military member can begin climbing the "in-processing" paperwork tower at the next base. Out-processing consists of retrieving medical records, turning in identification

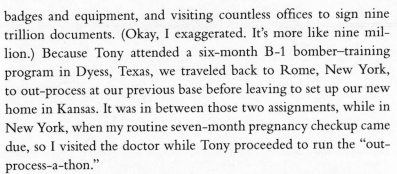

badges and equipment, and visiting countless offices to sign nine trillion documents. (Okay, I exaggerated. It's more like nine million.) Because Tony attended a six-month B-1 bomber–training program in Dyess, Texas, we traveled back to Rome, New York, to out-process at our previous base before leaving to set up our new home in Kansas. It was in between those two assignments, while in New York, when my routine seven-month pregnancy checkup came due, so I visited the doctor while Tony proceeded to run the "out-process-a-thon."

This medical detour put new obstacles between Tony and Wichita. Calls to previous and new commanders determined our alternate route. Tony hurdled the first challenge: we would live in a temporary living facility (TLF) in New York.[1] Tony then tunneled through the second barricade when his previous commander created a temporary position for him in his former squadron, which allowed Tony to remain in New York. He would not need to leave me while he fulfilled his military duties at the next base or have to inconvenience a relative to take his place at my side. The final obstacles disappeared when Tony's new commander, Colonel Tom, graciously assured Tony that he would hold his B-1 spot *and* our base home until we arrived. The Air Force family's blanket of care overwhelmed us.

The one word that best describes my month of bed rest is *casseroles*. When I hear this word, I do not envision dishes filled with

---

1. A temporary living facility is basically a hotel room with a kitchen for military families who just arrive or are leaving for their next assignment and need somewhere to stay temporarily.

noodles and sauces of every variety. I think of God's provision for the challenges in my life. The word triggers thoughts of how self-less friends shoveled our snowdrift-covered sidewalk. The friend would add just before leaving, "By the way, my wife made you this casserole." I think of the busy mom who picked up my eighteen-month-old numerous times for playdates so I could rest. Once I awoke from an accidental ten-minute nap and found the couches, chairs, carpet, and myself covered with craft glue and pieces of colored construction paper. Nico proudly exclaimed, "Mommy, looky what I made!" The thought of accidently falling asleep again while my eighteen-month-old toddler roamed free worried me, so I asked a friend to watch him. When my friend dropped off Nico, she would casually say, "I made an extra casserole, so don't worry about dinner tonight."

Military wives whom I had never met got wind of our predicament. They brought over their children's books and toys to share with my son, and somehow a casserole would mysteriously appear on the counter. These women created lovely dinners for a family they did not know. The word *casserole* makes me think of powerful military leaders who led with compassion as they created a job for my husband, giving us security while we faced the unforeseen challenge that God foreknew.

As spouses, we don't know what challenges lie before us on our military journey. We don't know what military or medical needs will prompt relocating to another new base, oftentimes partnered with a new culture. We don't know when a close military friend will receive orders and uproot from our lives. We don't know when one world power will threaten another and upset our family's security, but God does, and He *always* provides casseroles to see us through.

Dear Lord, I don't know what the future holds, but you do. Thank you for going out before me to assure that I am cared for no matter what the circumstance. Please put the individuals needing your care in my path so that I can display your love through my "casseroles."

WHAT CHALLENGES DO YOU CURRENTLY FACE? Are you trudging through an obstacle course of family, health, or work-related barriers? In what ways can you lessen your worries by turning to God? What kinds of "casseroles" can you give others to help them through their tough times?

FOUR

There I Was

The First Combat Mission

*Those who hope in the Lord will renew their strength.
They will soar on wings like eagles; they will run and not
grow weary, they will walk and not be faint.*

Isaiah 40:31

I put on my flight suit and headed for the B-52 bomber that awaited
with fifty-one 750-pound bombs loaded and ready for my first
combat mission. The plan was to launch as a four-ship formation of
B-52s to destroy an oil facility deep in enemy territory. The long
flight required that our four B-52s refuel in midair using other
aircraft.

As we approached Iraq that night, we descended to evade enemy
fighter aircraft. Once level at four hundred feet, we discovered that
our terrain avoidance (TA) system[2] and night vision goggles (NVGs)

---

2. A terrain avoidance system is a radar system that provides a picture of hazards
in front of an aircraft's flight path.

were ineffective while flying over the desert and through the thick fog. The TA and NVGs allow pilots to fly at low altitude, making it difficult for fighters' weapon systems to target us. During that mission, we found that the TA set was not effective with flat terrain. Furthermore, the NVGs required a clear night for them to function. Both devices typically used in training were practically useless. As a result, we flew off of a simple altimeter[3] reading, with no assistance to see terrain or obstacle changes in front of us. This was dangerous, but this was war.

Our system limitations forced us to use a map to maneuver around a tower near the target, which caused us to be slightly wide of the target area. As a result, we decided to withhold our weapons. Our aircrew did not want to deploy bombs unless we were completely confident of our target. We coordinated with airborne command and control assets to perform a racetrack (re-attack) while at low altitude to accomplish our mission.

When we returned to the target area, things quickly became intense. Two US aircraft had released weapons near our target; therefore, the enemy was aware of an impending attack. At five seconds prior to weapons release, I felt our large weapon bay doors begin to open as the target appeared through the fog. We were right on target. Out the corner of my eye, I spotted Triple-A (antiaircraft artillery) and red tracers[4] tracking toward us from the ground.

---

3. An altimeter is an instrument that measures altitude, or the height above the ground.
4. Red tracers are ammunition that can be observed in flight by their trails of smoke.

I called out, "Triple-A, three o'clock." The other pilot shouted, "Triple-A, nine o'clock." The enemy was shooting at us from both directions. We stayed on target. After our weapon bay doors opened completely, our aircraft began shaking violently as the fifty-one 750-pound bombs released.

My vision was temporarily blinded by a bright outside light as a huge explosion took place around me. The enemy stopped shooting. Seconds later, as the weapon bay doors closed, our electronic warfare officer ordered us to maneuver low to the ground, for the enemy had launched a missile and it was heading directly for us. My aircraft commander quickly dove his plane as close to the ground as possible, while simultaneously dropping countermeasures.[5]

Our B-52 achieved negative flight (which is the same feeling you get during the drop on a roller coaster ride) as we descended quickly toward the ground. The navigator yelled out, "Climb! Climb!" as I noticed the radar altimeter plummet to fifty feet! Our vulnerable B-52 aircraft, nearly half the length of a football field, was doing its best to duck, as if we were elephants playing dodgeball.

Have you ever met someone who shared their feeling of time slowing down during a time of crisis? I experienced such an event that night. It was apparent that we were about to hit the ground, and as I pulled back on the yoke—the control stick of the aircraft—only one thing was on my mind. It was not the beautiful love of my life,

---

5. The countermeasures are chaff and flares. Chaff are strips of metal, foil, or glass fiber with a metal content, usually dropped from an aircraft, used to reflect electromagnetic energy as a radar countermeasure. A flare is a device that produces a bright light.

Penny, waiting for me at our cozy home, or my loving parents in Brooklyn, New York, as they gathered around the table for home-cooked Italian meals. It was not my firstborn son, Nico, smiling and saying his familiar phrase, "Juko Nuko, Daddy" (translation: "Juice for Nico, Daddy"). It was not that I was about to die. No, I had only one thought: *I was at peace with God.* I completely trusted that He would not abandon me; thus, I was ready for whatever came my way—even death.

The engineers claim that we did not hit the ground because our aircraft experienced ground effect, a phenomenon where a cushion of air is compressed between the wing and the ground, but I believe that God placed His mighty hand under our aircraft and declared, "Not yet." The missile overshot us, and we survived our first combat mission.

That night we were diverted to a base when a missile hit one of the other B-52s and we experienced engine fire indications. We had to shut down two of our engines, but we made it back safely, and I thanked God and kissed the ground when we landed.

I was ecstatic to be alive. Trusting in God and believing that your salvation is secure requires faith. For me, the best example of faith is that of a child. If you ask a one-year-old to jump into your arms, she will jump without hesitation knowing that you will catch her. I trusted completely that God was in control—complete control. As a result, when I thought my life on this planet was about to end—I mean, I thought it was over—I did not worry. I was secure in my faith and believed in my soul that God would not abandon me.

After that night, I thanked God for preserving my life and vowed not to waste it. I promised to serve Him and never forget the joy of life. Every day since that night has been a bonus. And I thank God for it!

Thank you, Lord, for the gift of life. Please help me to never forget that I have today to make a positive difference in this world. Help me to remember the joy of life and the gift of salvation that comes through your son, Jesus.

DO YOU APPRECIATE LIFE or do you take it for granted? Right now, what is the most important challenge you face? Do you think you are in control? Are you at peace with God? Have you surrendered your anxieties to Him?

FIVE

Guess What, Mom? I'm Signing Up!

Surrendering Our Children to the Lord

He will cover you with his feathers, and under his wings you will find refuge; his faithfulness will be your shield and rampart. You will not fear the terror of night, nor the arrow that flies by day . . . For he will command his angels concerning you to guard you in all your ways.

Psalm 91:4–5, 11

"Mom, I'm going to join Army ROTC, and I want to go Rangers!"[6] my newly high school emancipated son announced as we strolled from the University of Central Missouri's student orientation to the parking lot. Antonio's diploma and stringy hat tassel still lay in the

---

6. ROTC is Reserved Officer Training Corps, a college-based military training program that prepares college students to become military officers. Rangers are "a highly trained and rapidly deployable light infantry force with specialized skills that enable it to engage a variety of conventional and Special Operations targets." See http://www.military.com/army-rangers/training.html. They are considered the Army's premier raid force.

backseat from last week's graduation, next to the half-empty bag of theater popcorn. "You're what?" I shrieked, wondering if a mom's "freaking out" voice was an insurance-covered category, just in case surrounding car windows shattered.

"Mom, I've *always* wanted to go into the Army—since I was little. I think it would be awesome having someone yell at me to get up and run each morning." I had to think back to the refreshments table. Did I see anyone lace the students' lemonade with delusion powder? I knew I should have led Antonio to the Greek Fraternities table before he caught sight of the Arnold Schwarzenegger-looking men in fatigues.

"Wait," I interrupted. "I've been shouting at you to get up since I bought your first backpack, crayons, and Buzz Lightyear lunch box. I can wear your dad's fatigues, buy a whistle, yell in a deep voice, and give you a toothbrush to clean your shower if that makes you feel better. You don't need to join the Army for that treatment. At least, think about joining the Air Force where it's safer. Not a ground force. And Rangers? Special Operations is more dangerous than the other Army regiments."

"Aww, Mom. I know this is right for me. You know that joining the Army is what I've *always* wanted to do."

My son was right. As soon as he could walk, he jumped from the fourth stair, sometimes landing on our unsuspecting saint of a dog. He routinely skydived from countertops and furniture. His preschool days kept my heart in constant fibrillation. At the time, I thought that if I could keep him alive until kindergarten, I would gain teacher reinforcements to help him survive until high school graduation.

As Antonio's age increased, so did his risk-taking adventures. One of the many houses we lived in included a balcony walkway overlooking the living room. I reprimanded him daily to stop inching along the ledge by his fingertips, which he usually did to evade chores. His idea of fun was camping without a tent, sleeping bag, or pillow. Grasshoppers living their grasshopper lives became hors d'oeuvres; unsuspecting turtles were roasted over open fires ignited by spinning two pieces of wood together. Had Missouri laws not prohibited skydiving until the age of eighteen, my Antonio would have jumped from planes at the age of six. To create a forever mother/son memory, Antonio and I jumped from a Cessna plane at fourteen thousand feet on the day he turned eighteen.

I sighed. Joining the Army fit him like his worn-out Puma shoes he refused to throw out, but how could I let him leave my protection? Who would tell him, "That's too high? Get down, or I'm taking your video games away?" How would I play fetch with him and his dog to prompt him to open up and talk when things bothered him? What if he witnessed terrible events that I could not shield him from? How would he get through war's trauma and remain healthy mentally and spiritually, not to mention avoid physical harm? Would he serve under noble commanders? These questions plague my thoughts and bring me to tears as I write, but I know the solution: I must release the momma-bear grip and surrender my child to God's protective arms. My career of raising my young child to become a God-loving, responsible adult is closing, and I must let go.

I mentioned Antonio's joining ROTC to a dear friend, who shared about the day her son was sworn into the Army:

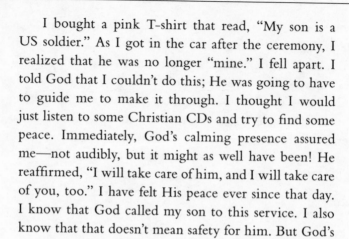

I bought a pink T-shirt that read, "My son is a US soldier." As I got in the car after the ceremony, I realized that he was no longer "mine." I fell apart. I told God that I couldn't do this; He was going to have to guide me to make it through. I thought I would just listen to some Christian CDs and try to find some peace. Immediately, God's calming presence assured me—not audibly, but it might as well have been! He reaffirmed, "I will take care of him, and I will take care of you, too." I have felt His peace ever since that day. I know that God called my son to this service. I also know that that doesn't mean safety for him. But God's care is better.

Our children are not our own. Parents with grown children will attest that even when potty training and teenage rebellion seem to drag on longer than the checkout line on Black Friday (i.e., forever), our children are walking across the high school graduation stage to receive a paper granting them passage into life's next stage. They are with us for a very short time. God lends us His children and gives us the honor to be called parents. Just as we marked out our individual paths in life, our sons and daughters will choose their direction. Some may receive the call to serve our country.

I admire my son for heeding God's call, wherever that may lead. I remind myself whenever worry rears its ugly head that God is the ultimate commander in chief and loves my son even more than I do. I am proud to be a military wife—and now, possibly a military mother—as I release my son from my meager arms and into God's all-powerful embrace.

Dear heavenly Father, although your care infinitely exceeds mine, it is tough surrendering my child to you. I'm used to being near to pick him up when he falls. Now I'm not there, so when my child is lonely or afraid, please remind him that you are the ultimate tower of strength. Shield him from danger, and let him rest in your protective embrace. Release me from worry's vise-like grip and allow your peace to reign in my family's life.

HOW DO YOU AVOID WORRYING about someone you love? What actions do you take to shield yourself from negative thinking? How can you encourage others to free themselves from fear and doubt? What specifically do you need to surrender to the Lord to experience peace for your daily life?

Resources

Learn more about the following organizations and websites in the Resources section in the back of this book.

- The Moms of Military Prayer and Support Group (MOMS) unites mothers across America and around the world in prayer for their children serving in the US military.

- *Go Army Parents* allows parents to share their thoughts, experiences, and questions about the US military in forums. Articles and weekly chat sessions are also offered.
- *Marine Parents* offers free services, connections, and outreach projects to support Marines and educate Marine moms, dads, spouses, families, and friends.
- *Navy for Moms* was created for the mothers (and loved ones) of those who are currently serving or considering serving in the US Navy. The site gives loved ones a place to discuss issues with others who share common concerns.
- *Not Alone* is a website that, in addition to several online military forums, offers Parent Group for parents and other family members to help them reestablish healthy relationships with returning warriors who have been touched by combat-related stress.

SIX

The Rabbi's Tattoos

Why We Fight

You will hear of wars and rumors of wars, but see to it that you are not alarmed. Such things must happen, but the end is still to come.

Matthew 24:6

As the elderly rabbi rolled up his sleeve, revealing tattooed numbers on his forearm, I knew this was a special man. It was a routine morning ride to high school on the B-train from Brooklyn to Manhattan and sitting beside me was a rabbi, fully garbed in a black hat and coat. He had a long white beard and two curly ringlets of hair that lightly brushed against each ear. We struck up a conversation, and he shared nuggets of wisdom that I have treasured to this day. The rabbi's tattoo was from a Nazi concentration camp where many of the rabbi's immediate family members had been slaughtered. He shared horrific stories of the atrocities that occurred in those camps.

After World War II, the rabbi dedicated his life to serving God and humankind. I will never forget the image of his tattooed forearm.

The rabbi's story reminds me why war is necessary. When good people close their eyes to wrongdoing and hope that others will take care of injustices, oppression and evil win. From what I have seen in my professional military career as a joint military officer, it is apparent to me that no one loathes war more than the soldier who must bear the awesome responsibility and consequences of war.

Many people have asked if I have problems as a Christian with having to kill if the situation requires it. I have been asked, "How can you be a Christian and kill?" As an Air Force bomber pilot who has dropped bombs in more than one war, I can say that it is challenging knowing that my actions probably resulted in people's deaths. However, I know that my actions were done professionally and to accomplish a greater good. When noble men do nothing, their inaction permits ruthless dictators and corrupt regimes to continue killing innocent people. When military servicemen and women use force to kill the enemy under certain criteria and situations, that choice is not taken lightly, but the action is necessary.

America's soldiers are volunteers who choose to fight for a greater good. We hope that our elected officials make wise decisions regarding when to use military power, but once their judgment is made, it is our responsibility to follow the lawful orders from the President of the United States down to our commanders on the ground. We are given commander's intent[7] and specific rules of engagement, and

___

7. Commander's intent is a concise expression of the purpose of the operation and the desired end state that serves as the initial impetus for the planning process. It may

then it is the responsibility of military professionals to create tactical plans that align with the commander's orders.

In my case, as a bomber pilot, it is my decision while flying to determine if my actions meet specific criteria such as rules of engagement, level of force, commander's intent, and target priority level. During my combat missions, decisions were always made in good conscience and targets were engaged with precision for the desired effect. On one mission, our crew intentionally withheld release of weapons on a target because we were not 100 percent sure of the target coordinates. We returned to our base with a full rack of weapons in order to avoid harming innocent people. It was the correct decision, and our leadership backed us up.

American servicemen are not robots who just do what we are told, nor are we warmongers. We are trained in the art of war and schooled in the rules of conflict. We are given specific rules of engagement that are general in nature, yet specific in execution. We are trained to use force proportionally and avoid use of excessive force. We obey the Geneva Convention, an international agreement designed to protect prisoners of war, even though many enemies have no care for common decency.

Some servicemen struggle with the idea that killing is against God's will. I disagree. It is clear throughout the Old Testament's history and in the New Testament's prophecy that war has and will continue to occur (see Matthew 24:6). The book of Revelation

---

also include the commander's assessment of where and how much risk is acceptable during the operation. (Milan Vego, "Operational Commander's Intent," http://www.ndu.edu/press/lib/images/jfq-57/vego-operationalCommanders.pdf)

forecasts battles and devastation. Wars will be with us, and it is the duty of military warriors to decide when and how to use force responsibly. Before engaging in battle, a warrior should ask himself: Is the use of force justifiable and measured? What is the motive of killing? Is it self-defense or unjustified, premeditated murder with evil intent?

For those completely against the notion of possibly harming or killing others in the service to your country, then perhaps a different career is in order. American servicemen have to trust our leaders to make the proper decision when they require us to unleash America's military power and sacrifice the blood of her troops. Once the decision is made, it is up to individuals to do their duty.

Numerous Department of Defense mental health clinics, organizations, and trained professionals are available to assist servicemen and women and combat veterans cope with this moral issue and the aftereffects of witnessing war. Several worthy organizations and resources are listed at the end of this chapter and again at the end of the book. Military chaplains are also a great source for returning war veterans. The military chaplains offer the privilege of confidentiality in nearly all circumstances (intent to harm oneself or others is the rare exception to confidentiality). Additionally, troops suffering from mental health challenges after conflict are often helped by their commanders, friends, and family. Relationships are key to recovery, and by being effective listeners, we can assist a fellow warrior in need.

The reason why servicemen and women fight is to defend the United States of America against all enemies, foreign and domestic.

It is through our sacrifices that America remains free and strong. We have an awesome responsibility to continue the fight against tyranny and do so with the hope that our actions are noble and true. We do not seek glory for doing our duty. We fight out of a sense of obligation to country and for our fellow soldier fighting alongside us. If we do not raise our arms to fight, then evil men and tyrants will threaten our existence. The image of the rabbi's tattooed arm reminds me that evil is real and must be confronted by good men, for there will always be "wars and rumors of wars" (Matthew 24:6).

Heavenly Father, as I perform my duty to defend my country, protect me and my fellow servicemen. Help me to seek your will to do what is right.

ARE YOU READY TO DEFEND AMERICA? What types of moral dilemmas have you or someone you know experienced? Have you considered or advised talking with a fellow serviceman, chaplain, or health care provider? If you are experiencing post-combat stress, what actions will you take to help yourself and those who love you?

Resources

Learn more about the following organizations and websites in the Resources section in the back of this book.

- Called to Serve Ministry is a military support site that discusses PTSD-related topics. The "R & R Room" offers encouragement, hope, and support through inspirational stories and related Scripture. On the site, spouses and warriors experiencing similar situations can encourage and pray for one another, and find helpful links to additional resources.

- Combat Faith provides Christian encouragement and education for military members wishing to strengthen their faith in God and veterans challenged with serious issues related to relationship struggles, substance abuse, and PTSD.
- *Day of Discovery*'s "The War Within: Finding Hope for Post-Traumatic Stress" is a four-part video series where veterans and their loved ones whose lives have been drastically changed by war will find encouragement.
- The Department of Defense established a twenty-four-hour, toll-free hotline number, (866) 966-1020, and two websites, afterdeployment.org and realwarriors.net, to help with PTSD and military-related challenges.
- Hopefortheheroes.com provides Christian help for PTSD. Daily messages of hope are delivered by phone, text, or e-mail.
- International Critical Incident Stress Foundation (ICISF) is a non-profit foundation dedicated to the prevention and mitigation of disabling stress. ICISF provides leadership, education, training, consultation, and support services in crisis intervention and disaster behavioral health services to the emergency response professions, other organizations, and communities worldwide.
- Military Ministry serves military members, veterans, and families through direct ministry and partnerships with chaplains, churches, and organizations. They offer marriage seminars, chaplain retreats, online devotionals, a prayer page,

rapid deployment kits, military support resources, and leadership training to equip churches to be "bridges to healing" for returning warriors, veterans, and their families.

- Military OneSource is a 24/7 resource that also offers three kinds of short-term, non-medical counseling options to active duty, guard, and reserve members and their families.

- The National Center for Post-Traumatic Stress Disorder, Department of Veterans Affairs, addresses the needs of veterans with military-related PTSD.

- NotAlone.com is a resource center and meeting room where warriors and spouses can confidentially meet online with other veterans and families for counseling and to discuss PTSD and other related topics with fellow veterans and family members.

- Point Man International Ministries' mission is to connect the hurting veteran, as well as their families and friends, to others who have already begun the transition home after war.

PART 2

Transition

SEVEN

Please Hear What I'm Not Saying

Taking Time to Listen

*Then you will call upon me and come and pray to me, and
I will listen to you.*

Jeremiah 29:12

"Help us move to Alabama, and we'll make it worth your while,"
Tony bribed. "Sounds awesome," our teenage friend eagerly replied,
since college tuition deadlines were fast approaching. "When do we
leave?" "Tomorrow," we said, hoping our answer didn't send him
running. Normally, we plan military relocations at length; however,
this particular move had an unforeseen kink: We fired the movers
after their first four hours on the job.

The relocation mayhem began with two dating movers yelling
obscenities at each other. As the harsh words transcended the garage
walls into the kitchen, Brie, my righteous four-year-old, questioned
why I did not put the movers on time-out. Several times, I politely
asked the quarreling couple to curb their cutting words. When they

moved their argument to the street, I curiously opened one of their packed boxes. I was shocked to discover a twenty-pound car battery charger balancing on top of Tony's hand-painted T-38, B-52, and B-1 plane models. I had spent months saving for the sentimental replicas of the planes that Tony had flown through the years. I slowly lifted the heavy battery. The relieved pressure triggered the cracked wings to separate from the plane's body and fall into the box's depth. I glanced up at the far wall. "No, they didn't!" I cried out loud. The garbage can, which had been full an hour ago, was empty. After searching several boxes, I located the trash—boxed and doubly sealed for extra protection. "Can I help, Mommy?" my brown-eyed nine-year-old, Antonio, asked, breaking through my frenzied emotions. "No, sweetheart. Thanks. Go play Nintendo. I've got it." I shrugged off his dejected look and returned to the issue at hand.

The last investigated garage box revealed family photos—ten years' worth. I had packed them in heavy plastic boxes, carefully labeled them by month and year, and secured them with packing tape for extra durability. When asked what I would save if my house caught on fire (after children and pets were safe) my blink instinct response is the family photos. My treasured memories were now out of sequence and spread beneath an opened dog food bag and a heavy, metal toolbox. Both items proved the photos' bending and oil-absorbing abilities. The empty photo containers were carefully boxed. Along with the meticulously packed garbage, the photo containers would remain safe from damage.

The miffed movers returned. Struggling to bridle my anger, I asked why they removed the organized photos from one carefully packed box and scattered them into another. They looked at each other as if I had asked them for the solution to global warming, and then answered in unison, "It's the rules. Anything packed by the owner must be repacked *professionally* [and they did emphasize *professionally*] by us, so our company won't be blamed if customers pack it wrong." I held my breath to stifle my sarcastic laugh from escaping.

While the lovebirds' packing errors continued to multiply in the garage, the living room crews were busy creating their own. I fearfully watched them hoist my beautiful ten-year anniversary gift, a baby grand piano, unprotected onto a cart. I frantically called our local music shop. They ordered me to stop the movers instantly and offered to transfer the piano themselves. When the newly hired sixteen-year-old mover defended his skill as a piano mover, since he attended a one-day training session the day before, I convinced him that the music company would give him and the others a needed break. He applauded the idea and began taking orders for lunch from his fellow workers.

While I was overseeing the piano-moving crisis, another mover emptied sand from the driveway basketball stand without my knowledge. I walked past my children, ignoring their pleas for attention, and entered the bedroom. A box of permanent markers had been freed from their protective carton and scattered in a garment box. Permanent black ink from an uncapped marker seeped onto my favorite pink angora sweater. I didn't ask this packer why he removed the ink pens from their secure box. Being a quick study, I understood his duty was to protect our possessions from our own unskilled packing abilities. Overwhelmed with the moving escapade, I ousted my kids to the neighbor's house so they would be out of the way. I never stopped to think how boxing up their treasures and the day's events distressed my little onlookers.

A base supervisor stopped by to inspect the packing. He informed us that no other movers were available to replace the A-Team assigned to us. We decided to rent a truck, move the household ourselves, and terminate the *professional* moving crew. Two sets of phenomenal neighbors helped us pack long after Taco Bell's closing time. Unfortunately the movers had the final word, even after they left. Our future tenant stopped by and parked his truck in our driveway. The wind picked up and the newly emptied, weightless basketball stand crashed onto the hood of our renter's shiny red truck.

One week later, I sighed at the same towers of brown boxes surrounding me, but now in the small Southern town of Deatsville, Alabama. I sidestepped the cardboard columns to find my twelve-year-old, Nico. Through the partially opened bedroom door, I glimpsed a brown tail thumping on the bed, as if nodding in agreement to my son's voice. I was ready to protest Nico allowing Rocky, our shedding chocolate lab, to sprawl out on the bed, but Nico's words froze my steps. I quietly inched away from his view. Tears welled in my eyes as I listened to my son's crackly voice saying to Rocky, "Don't worry. I know it's hard to move to another place, especially where they don't talk the same as us. I wish Dad wasn't in the military either, Rocky, but you will make new dog friends. I promise. I'll help you. In one year, we'll move again, but you will be okay because I'll never leave you. Never!" I watched a young, worried boy look into his dog's golden eyes, receiving comfort as he worked through his anxious feelings.[8]

---

8. I recount this story in my book *Choose to Dance* (Longwood, FL: Xulon, 2008).

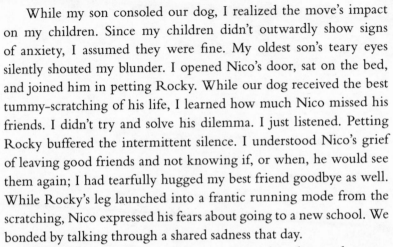

While my son consoled our dog, I realized the move's impact on my children. Since my children didn't outwardly show signs of anxiety, I assumed they were fine. My oldest son's teary eyes silently shouted my blunder. I opened Nico's door, sat on the bed, and joined him in petting Rocky. While our dog received the best tummy-scratching of his life, I learned how much Nico missed his friends. I didn't try and solve his dilemma. I just listened. Petting Rocky buffered the intermittent silence. I understood Nico's grief of leaving good friends and not knowing if, or when, he would see them again; I had tearfully hugged my best friend goodbye as well. While Rocky's leg launched into a frantic running mode from the scratching, Nico expressed his fears about going to a new school. We bonded by talking through a shared sadness that day.

The Alabama move gifted me with more than damaged possessions. I discovered the value of listening and the harm of preoccupation. I learned the importance of providing opportunities to talk, no matter if life pitches a mini-crisis, an all-out catastrophe, or just a normal day. When all seems calm on the outside, a flow of emotions may be raging underneath. During moves, I remind my kids (and myself) that the Lord understands everything we experience and remains in control. After all, who knew more about living out of a suitcase, making new friends, and battling acceptance than Jesus?

Now two of my three children attend college, but during those earlier moves, I learned to include my children in the moving process. Our family met, and jobs were assigned. I loaded their cupped hands with labels to brand their own boxes. One person acted as the dog commander and packed bowls and leashes. Another child maintained the movies, assuring DVDs and video games were set aside. Trash cans *never* again remained in the same area as the packing crew. Going-away parties allowed children to say goodbye to all their friends at once, exchange phone numbers, and plan future reconnections.

If anyone says that transitioning to a new location is easy, I challenge them to a polygraph test. These steps helped with moving, but most importantly, when I sense something is troubling one of my children, I find physical activities to trigger conversation. To this day, a game of fetch with our dog never fails to launch my boys into talking. When my daughter shops, her anxieties unfold like those encapsulated, tiny animal-shaped sponges that grow tenfold when placed in water. I've learned that solutions offered are not as important as an ear to hear. As Francis D. Drucker so eloquently stated, "The most important thing in communication is to hear what isn't being said." Just being available assures them that I care, regardless if they choose to talk or not.

Lord, help me to listen to the unspoken words. Nudge me to take "time-outs" when life's busyness tries to steal away family time. Help me to focus on the important things in life: you, my spouse, my children, family, and friends.

WHAT ACTIVITIES AND COMMITMENTS fill your planner? What enjoyable activities launch conversation in your family? Are those activities on your daily "to-do" list?

Resources

The Military Family Network website offers a great relocation guide for before, during, and after moves. Armed Forces Crossroads website is dedicated to those members and their families and friends who are separated. Learn more about these websites in the Resources section in the back of this book.

EIGHT

Old Lady on the Train

God's Predestined Plan

In his heart a man plans his course, but the Lord determines his steps.

Proverbs 16:9

My mom knew that someday I would be a pilot. She shared that as a child, I would always look up for airplanes. As a teenager, I attended Aviation High School, located more than an hour away from home by train, so I could learn everything about airplanes. Instead of a football stadium, Aviation High School had a hanger filled with jet aircraft and helicopters. During my junior year, a guest United States Air Force Academy cadet spoke to my class. The proud cadet explained that the Air Force Academy is the only school in the country guaranteeing graduates a pilot training slot, even if they did not have 20/20 vision (that is, as long as vision was correctable to 20/20). Since my vision was not 20/20, the Air Force Academy was my gateway to my dream job of flying jets for the US Air Force.

After reading the brochure, I knew where I belonged. The Academy encouraged a blend of academic, athletic, and leadership excellence. I was president of the student body, editor of the yearbook, a Boy Scout, a cadet in the Civil Air Patrol, and a lettered member of the track and field team. I was focused on achieving my goal and believed nothing would stop me. I refused to apply to other colleges because I was going to the Air Force Academy to learn how to fly jets. Failure was not an option, until . . .

The Air Force Academy rejected my admissions application because of my average SAT scores. I was devastated. But just three days later, something unbelievable happened on the B-train subway that altered my life flight path forever.

While returning home from school on the crowded train, I noticed an elderly lady standing nearby. My father raised me to offer ladies my seat, so I got up and offered the lady the empty spot. She appreciatively accepted my offer. I could tell from her accent and broken English that she was Italian, and we changed from speaking English to our native tongue. That is when it happened. She noticed that my yellow and green jacket resembled her son's high school jacket. She explained that her son, Salvatore, was now an Air Force F-15 fighter pilot, and each year he visited from Japan. "In fact," she said with a smile, "he arrived just the other day and is home for a few days." She continued, "Because you are such a nice boy and offered me your seat, why not visit him tonight? Maybe he could help you? You remind me so much of him."

That night I met Sal and discovered he was the son of Italian immigrants too. English was his second language, he had attended

Aviation High School, and coincidentally he had not been accepted to the Air Force Academy initially due to his SAT scores. He shared how he had attended Northwestern Preparatory School in Santa Barbara, California, to boost his SAT scores, which led to his acceptance at the Air Force Academy. Sal called the president of Northwestern Preparatory School that very night and helped get me admitted— with one small catch. The cost of attending this six-month prep school was seven thousand dollars.

During our traditional family meal that evening, I shared all that transpired, and my mom thought it was a miracle or *La forza del signore* ("power of God"). My dad, an electrician who was about to purchase his first new car, gave me the money to pursue my dreams instead. In June of 1982, I went to Santa Barbara to enter the coliseum of life and battle against thousands of vocabulary words and hundreds of frivolous math tests. After six months, I improved my SAT score by 40 percent. I reapplied and was accepted to the Air Force Academy. The six months of focused study paid off, and I was on my way to fulfill my dream to fly jets. What a ride!

Have you ever watched the scene from *Rocky II* after Rocky defeats the heavyweight champion of the world? He throws the large belt buckle over his shoulder and passionately yells, "Yo, Adrian, I did it!" Well, magnify that by a thousand and you will have a flavor of the joy I experienced after achieving my goal. It rocked my soul. The whole experience defined my life and taught me how to achieve success.

Success is the result of hard work, determination, and a little bit of "luck" (not pure happenstance, but God providing opportunities), and it begins with knowing what you want. Bomber pilots train to hit a target, and we spend lots of time planning each mission prior to flight in order to do so. We identify our desired impact point and angle of attack. We take into account threats, weather, and system limitations. The target is our primary focus—the mission is designed around it. Without a target, bomber pilots have no significance and would serve no purpose.

Many servicemen are uncertain of their personal "targets" and spend a majority of their time ineffectively as a result. It is imperative that you stop the busyness and take time to think about what you want out of life so you can achieve your goals. When you are able to fuse your talents with your passion, and ideally make a living doing what you love, then you will have identified your primary target.

Once you know what you want, achieving your goal requires good old fashioned hard work. I am the son of Italian immigrants and learned English in elementary school. My family went through tough times when I was a child, and I recall one time when we had to literally break our family piggy bank to put food on the table. Life was challenging, but we made it. My dad was laid off once, but he refused to accept unemployment. He kept looking for a job until he found one. If my father and mother "made it" in America without knowing the language and customs, how much more should I? America is the land of opportunity. God blesses us with so many natural resources and a government that encourages innovation and free enterprise. We are fortunate to live in America. Through the power of ideas and with the opportunity afforded us as Americans, we can follow our ambitions and live our dreams. The key is to know what you want and then to go out and make it happen.

Knowing who you are and what you want to achieve makes life meaningful. Conversely, not knowing your primary target is like taking off on a bomber mission and wandering aimlessly, which makes no sense. However, when your target is pinpointed, you can work toward achieving your dreams. And there is no better place on earth than America to live your dreams. You will have to overcome many obstacles along the way, including thunderstorms and other unforeseen hazards, but not giving up (determination) and navigating though the storms of life (focus) will get you to the target.

In the Air Force, we call hitting the target a "shack." In order to shack a target, everything has to go right, and I mean everything. That's where luck fits in. Some people believe in luck, or coincidence in their favor. However, I believe in a higher power and that God has His hands in coincidences somehow. It is a mystery of faith to believe that God gets involved in our lives, but I trust that He does! The old lady on the train, in my opinion, was God providing a path for my success. I had to show up, work hard, and be determined to succeed. My parents had to risk giving me money and sending me away on my own. But, had it not been for that old lady on the train, who knows how my life would have played out?

In my heart I planned my goal of flying jets for the Air Force, but it was God who linked the dots allowing me to achieve my dream. I believe God predestined me to meet that old lady on the train and to be where I am right now. He provided a gateway for me to experience the desires of my heart. Now I am able to share my passions and life experiences with the hope of encouraging others to trust in God and to use their talents to serve Him and others. I just had to show up and believe. It was God's predestined plan.

Life is full of possibilities and surprises. We all go through various transitions in our lives. If you are preparing for transitions, then find time to think and pray about what you want your target to be. Spend quality time reflecting on your talents and passions, then focus on your specific target and get to work. Develop plans for achieving your dreams and trust in the Lord to do the rest. Aim higher!

Heavenly Father, give me the inner strength to persevere during trials. Give me discernment to determine what path to take.

WHAT ARE YOUR PASSIONS AND TALENTS? Have life's events taken you on an uncharted path? What is your target? Are you open to new career paths? How are you working daily toward achieving your goals?

NINE

There's a Toilet in My Hallway

Finding Blessings during Tough Times

May the God who gives endurance and encouragement give you a spirit of unity among yourselves as you follow Christ Jesus.

Romans 15:5

My husband had just left for a TDY[9] to somewhere in the Middle East—that's all I knew. The spouses of the deployed were invited to meet at the commander's home for an informational meeting. After the meeting, I picked up my son, Nico, from a friend's house and returned to my base home at Griffiss AFB in Rome, New York. As I walked toward Nico's room, a strange silhouette stood in my darkened hallway. It was too short to be an intruder. As I inched closer, a white figure appeared. Was that my . . . toilet? My heart raced. *What*

---

9.   TDY is a temporary duty assignment somewhere other than the permanent duty station. These assignments can last from one day up to numerous months.

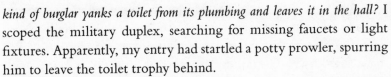

kind of burglar yanks a toilet from its plumbing and leaves it in the hall? I scoped the military duplex, searching for missing faucets or light fixtures. Apparently, my entry had startled a potty prowler, spurring him to leave the toilet trophy behind.

I noticed a formal looking document on the table from Civil Engineering (CE). CE manages military housing matters. When living on base, families are subjected to CE entering when the resident is gone to resolve serious maintenance problems. Apparently, a neighbor's septic system had gone awry, and diagnosing the problem involved examining neighboring plumbing units. Mine, for some unknown reason, was left to decorate the hallway. The challenging feat of potty training my toddler took a new twist. After weeks of treat and toy bribery to shift Nico off the potty chair and onto the big boy toilet, I now had to explain, in two-year-old dialect, why pottying in the hallway toilet was off limits. It would be a long evening.

The hallway toilet incident marked the first item in a lengthy list that fell under the first rule of the Spouses' Laws of TDY, which states that immediately after a military spouse leaves TDY, anything and everything that can possibly go wrong will. In my husband's deployment history, Nico came down with a severe case of chicken pox—the same week of the toilet episode. When stationed in Kansas, Nico played in the neighbor's backyard with the Wichita clouds abnormally swirling above his head. I sprinted for Antonio's baby formula, and then hustled Nico into our neighbor's basement until the threatening tornado disappeared. At three years of age, Brie microwaved my only phone and decided that painting smiley faces with red fingernail polish would brighten up my brand-new white-striped bed comforter. On my son Antonio's eighth birthday, we sang him "Happy Birthday" while taking shelter underneath a bed mattress from a party-crashing tornado, this time in Missouri. Once, a mechanic neglected to fully tighten the lug nuts on a repaired tire that decided to flatten an hour after my husband was airborne, nearly making me a death statistic. Many more episodes, too numerous to count, stock the "woe-is-me" warehouse.

Every spouse I know owns a pantry of perils. When we gather, we dust off the mishaps and nod our heads knowingly, for spouses *feel* each other's challenges. This leads to the second law of TDY: Military friendships form quickly in calamity and, more often than not, last forever. In a crisis, spouses are mamma bears protecting one another. Catch a virus? They clean your home, babysit your kids, and haul you to the doctor. Car breaks down? They rescue you, and then find an available repairman—usually some unsuspecting, un-deployed husband. Principal called because a child's in trouble? They listen, love, and support. Lonely? They reschedule appointments, shelve their plans, and carve time out of their schedules to be available. Military life is friendship Velcro; it uniquely bonds friends—for life.

I am happy to conclude that my duplex neighbor shared her toilet and another neighbor lent me her phone. Our friendships grew as a result. The chicken pox rash actually sped up potty training because wet diapers plus an open rash equals *ouch*! My Wichita neighbor dispelled panic and created positive memories by strumming his guitar, singing, and playing games with his family, Nico, and me. The comforter was reversible, and thankfully, the Missouri tornado limited its damage to my ancient patio furniture, which I had wanted to replace for years. A military friend followed me to safety and helped me fix my loose tire. As I look back, all the temporary mishaps left a trail of unexpected blessings—the greatest of these being the selfless friends God provided when the going got tough.

Lord, please place friends in my life to strengthen me during challenging times. Help me to encourage others daily and to recognize their needs.

WHAT TDY MISHAPS HAVE YOU EXPERIENCED? In what ways did friends help during these challenging times? How can you help smooth the path when rocky challenges confront others?

Resources

Christian Military Wives is a multi-denominational, Bible-based ministry of Christian Military Fellowship and was established to assist military wives and their families. Called to Serve Ministry is a support website for both spouses and warriors, offering discussion forums, encouraging stories, and prayer support. Military SOS (Significant Other Support) and Milspouse.com are support and information resources for military spouses of all branches around the world. Learn more about these organizations and websites in the Resources section in the back of this book.

TEN

Give Me My Sunglasses

Balancing Family and Career

*Train a child in the way he should go, and when he is old
he will not turn from it.*

Proverbs 22:6

"Penny, we have to be strong when dropping off Nico at the airport today, so don't cry," I stated in a military tone, as if briefing soldiers for an upcoming mission. Nico, at the time only fourteen years old, was on his way to London, England, to attend a boarding school, since my remote overseas assignment did not have a local English-speaking high school. The thought of our close family being separated devastated us; however, we made the best of it. Although costly, we would fly two weekends a month to visit. We reasoned that Nico had an outgoing personality and adapted to change easily. He understood my military obligation and that this separation was part of our family's service to country.

I was doing my best to be the man of the house, and I wanted my wife to be strong too, to refrain from crying in front of Nico to assure him that we were at peace with this decision. As we piled into our minivan for the dreaded airport drive, I looked back in my rearview mirror and for a split second I envisioned Nico as a two-year-old in his car seat.

I looked at his strong blue eyes and smiled. I could not believe how quickly the years had flown by. Then something completely unexpected occurred, as if the leaning tower of Pisa tipped over. From out of nowhere, I started crying. I quickly wiped my tears and did my best to mask my emotions. I turned on the stereo and asked Penny to get my sunglasses. She asked why I needed sunglasses on an overcast day. "Just give me my sunglasses, please," I said, and that is when she noticed my tears. She shook her head in disbelief as if to say, "You gotta be kidding me!" I could see that she was amused that "Mr. Tough Guy," who had just recited a "don't cry briefing," was now breaking protocol.

Penny and I would replay that same scene years later when Nico left home to attend Azusa Pacific University in California. Déjà vu occurred as I entered the cab after leaving him in his dorm room. I needed my sunglasses again as I told the cab driver, "Just drive!" Letting go is not easy, but it is necessary. After we brought Nico to college, he called and gave me a dose of encouragement. He said, "Dad, I just want to thank you for serving our country all these years and for being my dad. I love you." I deeply appreciated his thoughtfulness.

During my career, I strived to balance career with family. I prioritized God first, then family, then job. I love my country and will serve her with all that I have, but my family takes precedence. For example, I gave my children all I had to give as a father and feel very little regret for how I raised them. I am confident that they will succeed in anything they pursue, and I am very proud of them. I do not regret the time I spent with them, or wish that I had spent that time working instead.

There are many warriors in the military who follow selfish ambitions and practically alienate themselves from their families. Their relationship with their spouse and children is practically nonexistent. You will find these people at the bar boasting about how great they are, and they expect others to join them as they drink their sorrows away. Many of these workaholics are so drunk with their profession and self that they lose sight of whom they should serve. These warriors prioritized themselves over their families instead of finding a balance.

Midway through my career, one such leader helped me understand this important challenge. Chief Master Sergeant Dale Buckingham, at the time the senior enlisted leader at Whiteman Air Force Base, asked me to stop by his office before leaving for Intermediate Service School (ISS).[10] While my family waited in the car with our bags packed, I went to visit him. He shared that he was retiring soon and that he had made a select amount of special gift coins and wanted me to have one. He asked me to place the coin somewhere I

---

10. ISS teaches middle management, leadership, and joint courses (understanding and working with other military branches). The top twenty percent of field grade officers (rank of major) are selected to attend ISS.

could see it. He said, "Every time you look at this coin, I want you to take care of yourself. You are always serving others, your unit and your family, but please take time for yourself too."

His message was for me to go fishing occasionally. Play golf. Take time off with family and friends. Cherish my children. I was amazed that this leader, at the culmination of his career, would give me such a message and honor me with this special gift. I have been given hundreds of special gift coins, but there is only one on my desk, and that is the coin from Chief Buckingham. I have treasured his wisdom and gift and will never forget his message.

Since that day, I have done my best to balance career, family, and self. Sure, I missed birthdays and soccer games due to service to country, but when faced with a choice of attending frivolous social meetings or my child's school Christmas recital, I chose family first. Whenever I was TDY for extensive periods of time, I chose to include my family in my service, bringing them along—safety permitting—so they could experience other cultures and we could stay united. Due to my strong Italian family culture, my parents raised me to value God and family over everything, so it has come somewhat natural to me to keep the family close. I do not regret those choices.

Our professional careers are important, but military service will suck everything out of us and then some if we let it. We can never give enough time to our jobs, for there will always be another important mission, another phone call that we have to take, and another meeting we need to attend. Some warriors are the first ones in to work and the last ones to leave, and they are proud of that fact, although their spouse and kids are left to fend for themselves. They volunteer for assignments and extra duties, all in the hopes of promotion or recognition, but at what price?

Chose your priorities now—don't tell yourself you'll adjust your priorities later. Spend time with your spouse. Go on dates and keep the passion alive. Be there for your kids, for in the blink of an eye, they will grow wings and fly away from the nest. If you raise them well, they will soar and make wise choices. Take the time now to be honest with yourself about your priorities. I am not advocating that you neglect doing your duty, but I am encouraging you to keep the big picture in mind and to find the proper balance between family and career.

Now that my children are older and embarking on their life journeys, I am satisfied with my decisions. The tears hidden behind my sunglasses on the day we drove Nico to the airport were tears of sorrow and joy. Sorrow for letting my son go, but sincere contentment for the wonderful memories of life with my family and career.

Lord, help me establish a balance between career and family. Give me wisdom to raise my children properly so they in turn will make wise choices in life.

HOW ARE YOU BALANCING family life with career challenges? Are you happy with how you prioritize your time? If not, what remedies are required? Do you have a strong relationship with your children? Are you cherishing each day with your loved ones? In what ways do you find time for yourself?

ELEVEN

Bella Italia! Now Let's Go Home

Adjusting to Foreign Military Relocations

Accept one another, then, just as Christ accepted you, in order to bring praise to God.

Romans 15:7

Kerplunk. A copper-colored Euro coin passed the sculpted muscular thighs and splashed into gushing water. A tanned Mediterranean woman in a fitted yellow sundress struggled to restrain her curious children from jumping in. *Plink* bounced a coin off the massive white-winged marble horse and into the rippling water reservoir below. *Kerplunk. Kerplink. Kerplunk.* The tossed coins landed like raindrops as one tourist after another launched them along with their wishes into Rome's Trevi Fountain. Each heart hoped to fulfill the ancient legend: A coin thrown over one's shoulder into Trevi Fountain guaranteed a return visit to Rome. I pushed my coins back into my pocket unnoticed. I did not want to return to Italy. Not after our initial traumatic experiences. I just wanted to return home to America.

Five days after landing at Aviano Air Base, we headed to the town that we would adopt as home. As we drove south to the medieval town of Ferrara, so did our luck. Tony was placed on two weeks of strict bed rest, and then was hospitalized for an acute medical condition that required surgery. Since I did not take my Italian driver's license test yet, I rode a borrowed bike every day to the city's highly acclaimed university teaching hospital. Though Tony's surgery was a success, he received no pain medications (because Italian doctors do not promote pain medicine) and required an additional week of bed rest. After searching several floors to locate the only wheelchair in the entire hospital (seriously, they had only one) and becoming trapped in an elevator that must have been built during the Renaissance era, we left the hospital with a new appreciation for America's health care. Now our family could move to phase two of our Italian journey: Finding a place to live.

While Tony rested in the small hotel room that our family had lived in for over a month, my mission evolved to moving the five of us—six counting our chocolate lab—into an apartment. Tony worked with the North Atlantic Treaty Organization (NATO) in Ferrara, and the closest American base housing was an hour and twenty minutes away in Vicenza. We would live in an Italian community, and my children would attend a 95 percent Italian international school.

I met with a realtor and attempted to converse while Tony recuperated. She patiently showed me several apartments. I questioned the barren kitchens. She explained that Italians take their kitchens with them when they move. Not only did we need to rent an apartment, we would have to buy an entire kitchen too!

After visiting a dozen kitchenless apartments, the thirteenth proved to be the winner. It was equipped with countertops, cabinets, and even a kitchen sink, a lucky find in many European countries. The realtor captivated my artistic side with the renovated condominium complex built in the 1400s. I time-warped back six hundred years as I strolled by the authentic frescos lining the stately thirty-foot-high arched entryway to the building. As I entered the kitchen overlooking a beautifully maintained rose garden and full-sized pool, I couldn't hand over the Euros fast enough. We had found our dream-come-true Italian abode—or so I thought.

While Tony rested at the hotel, I passed the Italian driving test, and then the kids and I journeyed back and forth, hauling luggage into our new home. It was a sultry day, so I baited the kids to finish their work with a pool swim reward. Phenomenally, the kids transformed their listless selves into powerhouse cleaners and scurried upstairs to change into their swimsuits.

While the kids were upstairs, the doorbell rang. A beautiful, middle-aged woman introduced herself in broken English as Tatiana; she lived in the apartment directly below ours. Cheerfully, I introduced myself and expressed how happy I was to move in. I thought to myself, *Wow! Italian hospitality so soon!*—until she moved on to her second sentence: "Whena will youa be moving outa?" Confused, I replied, "Two years or more. Why?" She retorted, "Because you needa to move outa soona. I noa canna hava youa living ona my heada with alla this noisea for two yearsa!" She growled something in Italian and stormed down the hall.

Shaken, I called the kids and took them to the condominium's pool. They had been cooped up in a hotel room for over a month, and they were excited to play. I needed to recover from Tatiana's "gracious welcome." The kids happily jumped off the diving board while I searched for a vacant chair.

As I surveyed the crowded pool area, I spotted Tatiana wasting no time, wildly gesturing toward me while talking to another woman who glared my way. I tried to brush off their scowls and found an empty chair, but as my 130 pounds met the plastic, it separated into four pieces. Without thinking, I shouted, "This day is unbelievable!" All eyes turned to the new *Americana* tenant.

A dark-haired, Adonis-type man sauntered toward me. In broken English, he explained that all tenants buy their own chairs. I had broken a neighbor's chair. He then iced his good news by announcing ". . . and from twelve o'clock until four o'clock is *riposa*, a time when Italians rest. Your children should not splash or make noise in the pool, since many people are sleeping." "Right," I thought. "I might as well tell my kids not to breathe!"

Through welling tears, I apologized and assured him that I would replace the broken chair and quiet my cabin fever kids. I looked across the pool to see Tatiana smiling smugly. I gathered my disgruntled kids and returned to the condo, only to find that after I became flustered with Tatiana's "neighborly welcome," I locked my house and car keys inside. I called Tony, who called our landlord, Leah, and translated the situation. She would immediately unlock the door when she got off work—in three hours!

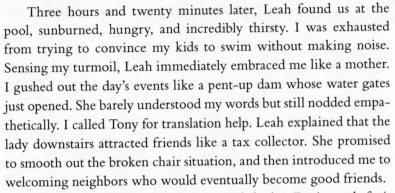

Three hours and twenty minutes later, Leah found us at the pool, sunburned, hungry, and incredibly thirsty. I was exhausted from trying to convince my kids to swim without making noise. Sensing my turmoil, Leah immediately embraced me like a mother. I gushed out the day's events like a pent-up dam whose water gates just opened. She barely understood my words but still nodded empathetically. I called Tony for translation help. Leah explained that the lady downstairs attracted friends like a tax collector. She promised to smooth out the broken chair situation, and then introduced me to welcoming neighbors who would eventually become good friends.

I learned the Italian cultural dos and don'ts: *Don't* touch fruit at the grocery store without gloves. *Don't* order cappuccino after 11:30 a.m. *Don't* wear shorts if you are over twenty years old or you are earmarked as a certified outsider. *Do* expect Italian friends to be at *least* an hour late to any engagement. *Do* drive during *riposa* because the streets are empty. *Do* expect the trains and schools to close because employees strike to get a day off. *Don't* expect businesses to be open in August when Italians travel on holiday—even if you are trying to get your electricity or phone services turned on!

After I opened myself up to cultural differences, I grew to love the Italian lifestyle. When the electrician arrived to repair our electric water heater, I welcomed his accompanying family for dinner. I looked forward to three-hour restaurant dinners. I offered our doctor *pranzo*, or lunch, when he dropped in unexpectedly to check up on my son's ear infection. Instead of refusing hospitality, I accepted the market vendor's offer that I pay the following week for flowers when I was short a few dollars. I allowed my children to play after midnight in the castle's piazza with other kids without fear of their abduction. I embraced the fact that no matter what time of day you dropped in on a friend, you were welcomed and fed like nobility.

I learned to love an unfamiliar culture that had initially frightened me. My Italian improved, and I met friends excited to learn English. I began a Bible study that included women from Syria, Denmark, Italy, and the United States. The Americans introduced the others to peanut butter, potlucks, theme-based birthday parties, and gifting homemade cookies at Christmas. (Tatiana was especially surprised to receive the treats, and even became friendly for a week.) The Europeans showed us the beautiful art of Italian living. We learned that despite our ethnic differences, love for God united us as one people. I realized that by embracing cultural diversity, rather than focusing on the differences, my kids and I had been showered in new and enriching experiences. As the end of Tony's assignment neared, I pleaded with him to extend our assignment one more year.

The final week before returning to America, I reflected on our Italian assignment. I recalled how my feelings had evolved from the first month in Italy to that moment and smiled. My Italian experience taught me to accept foreign cultures, to give them a chance instead of passing judgment, *to love my neighbor as myself*, even when that neighbor spoke a different language. Had I remained closeminded I would have missed out on wonderful friendships and rich Italian traditions.

I reached deep into my pockets and retrieved a handful of coins. I tossed them one by one, making sure each one landed smack in the middle of Rome's breathtaking Trevi Fountain. I now look forward to the day I can return to a country that I consider home.

Dear Lord, thank you for the experiences military life offers. Help me to see the positive in every transition while I experience new friends, cultures, and locations.

HOW HAS RELOCATING STRENGTHENED YOU? What trying experiences can you look back on and laugh about? What can you do beforehand to mentally prepare yourself and your family for a positive transition to a new location?

TWELVE

EOS No More

Preparing for Change

No man has power over the wind to contain it.

Ecclesiastes 8:8

There will come a time in your military service when you feel ready to change career fields. After serving over twenty years on active duty, the time seemed right for something new. The economy was doing well and there were lots of job opportunities. I reasoned that I could start a second career while still relatively young. Flying jets for the Air Force was my childhood dream come true, so giving up my dream job was the hardest decision I have had to make. I met with many mentors and advisors who recommended I stay in the military, but ultimately it was my choice.

Flying an advanced supersonic jet aircraft in formation a few feet from another aircraft was the thrill of a lifetime. Cranking and banking in a T-38, and dropping bombs on target and on time in a B-2 stealth bomber was exhilarating. As a Senior Service School candidate, I was in a position to make the rank of colonel. However, accepting the advancement required two moves in three years. My children would have to attend three different high schools, as my oldest son had already done. As military members, we understand that we are not the only ones serving our country, but our families serve as well. However, I felt my children had served their country well and deserved to finish high school with their friends. After careful consideration and prayer, I retired and was hired as a pilot by Delta, Continental, and EOS Airlines. I chose EOS, because I saw a future with a new, growing company and the pay was good.

Flying Boeing 757s from New York City to London was a blast and the team of EOS pilots was outstanding. A new dream job! I made good money, plus retirement pay, until . . . one morning I checked the online work schedule for the following week. As the computer screen blinked to life, it revealed an e-mail stating that EOS had declared bankruptcy. My jaw hit the floor, and I informed Penny of the shocking news. She thought I was joking until she read the e-mail herself. This situation was beyond my control. Just like that, EOS was no more! Now what?

Rather than wallow in self-pity and second-guess my decision to retire, I needed to work. Clebe McClary, an amazing motivational speaker and wounded Vietnam veteran, has a great saying when it comes to tough times. In a thick Alabama drawl, he encourages individuals facing challenges to "FIDO," which stands for "forget it and drive on." I completely agree with his philosophy and decided to maintain a positive attitude. Penny found a job as a school nurse and I worked at my family business.

Years earlier, Penny, my brother Giuliano, and his wife, Barbara, started an Italian restaurant called Monetti's Pizzeria Ristorante. Without any flying jobs open, I rolled up my sleeves and worked at the restaurant. It was a humbling experience to one minute be flying a Boeing 757 aircraft while eating caviar and staying at exotic hotels, and the next delivering pizzas, washing dishes, and making pizza dough. Giuliano chided me and said, "Bro, you used to be in the Air Force, but now I am going to make you a Marine!"

After a year at Monetti's restaurant, other opportunities sprouted up and Science Applications International Corporation (SAIC) offered me a position as a combat analyst. After a few months on the new job, my former Air Force commander informed me of a new Air Force initiative to return retired pilots to active duty due to a pilot shortfall. The upside was that my family would remain at our present base. We would not move, so my children would continue attending the same schools. The downside was that promotions were off-limits.

My initial thought was to say no. I had a good-paying job with SAIC and was still helping the Air Force as a contractor. However, over Memorial Day weekend, while watching a program about airmen transporting heroes' caskets from the war zone to their final resting places, the message hit home that a war still waged on. I brought my family together and expressed my renewed calling to serve our country. Now, for a few more years, I once again fly the B-2 stealth bomber and teach young pilots to fly and fight with the B-2.

I never thought that I would see active duty again after retiring. Each day's adventures await discovery. You just have to show up and do your best. One hero who showed up and did his best daily in service to America reminded me of the importance of living life fully and appreciating freedom. As a cadet at the Air Force Academy, I met a wonderful man named Robbie Risner. This Air Force hero had been tortured and held captive for seven years in Vietnam. Brigadier General Risner shared that while he lived three years in solitary confinement, he spent extended periods of time in darkness. A small beam of light would filter in through the door's crack when he was given meals. This gifted him with hope. I cherish a saying he wrote down and signed for me, "You can't whip a man that won't quit."

What impacted me the most about his story was when he described the joy he felt when feeling the rain. After being released from captivity, Robby Risner prepared to return home. He received new clothes and finally had the opportunity to clean himself. As he left the hospital to board the bus, it began to rain. Others in the group ran for cover, but Robbie Risner walked into the middle of the street and cried tears of joy as the rain hit his face. He shared that for years, he yearned for freedom and waited for the day he would feel the wetness of rain again. I cannot express in words what his story and perspective meant to me.

Whenever life rains challenges on me, I think of Robbie Risner raising his face toward the heavens in the rain, and that thought keeps my life in perspective. My passion has evolved from not only flying jets, but also encouraging others. As a motivational speaker, I use the acronym *FLY* to remind people to always look *F*orward, *L*ove life and live it fully, and to say *Y*es to new opportunities.

Forward. Too many people live in the past and focus on decisions they regret, rather than looking forward. They hold grudges against others and constantly complain about how unfair their life has been. Focusing on the past is like picking a scab. The scratching initially relieves the annoyance, but in time, the scab bleeds from the irritation. Sometimes the itching can cause infection. Do not infect yourself and others by dwelling on regrets. Instead, always look forward to new possibilities and adventures. It is all a matter of perspective on how you choose to see things. I know it is not easy, but it can be done—you have to choose to look forward.

Love Life and Live it Fully. Take time to discover what your desires are and devote energies toward achieving your dreams. Life is rewarding, particularly when you help others and achieve your goals. As military men and women, we are called to serve something bigger than ourselves, our country. As a result, we have rewarding jobs and responsibilities. We are lucky to live a life of service and meaning. However, I encourage you to *aim higher still.* Live each day as if it were your last and encourage others to live life fully too. Use your God-given talents to make a positive difference in your family, workplace, and community.

Yes. Say yes to new opportunities and challenges as they arise. Go dancing. Try ice-skating. Hike Mount Sinai. Ride a horse. Have fun. Who knows what tomorrow may bring? Life is too short to use the words, "I wish I would have . . ." Instead, say, yes more often than you say no. Try it. You may like it. As the Scriptures say, rather than wasting time uselessly grasping at the wind to contain it (Ecclesiastes 8:8), enjoy the breeze and fan the winds of success. Choose to *FLY* when you face life-changing decisions. Embrace those challenges and welcome the new adventure with a positive attitude.

Heavenly Father, as I prepare for change, be with me and provide mentors and friends to help me make the best decision. Help me to choose wisely and to maintain a positive attitude about upcoming challenges.

JUST BECAUSE WE ARE CHRISTIANS doesn't mean bad things won't happen. Are you contemplating retiring or starting a new career? Describe your attitude when things do not go as planned. Do you blame others or do you view problems as challenges to overcome?

Resources

See "Support for Veterans Transitioning into the Civilian Workforce" in the Resources section in the back of this book.

THIRTEEN

When the Honeymoon Is Over

Life After Deployments

*Make my joy complete by being like-minded, having the
same love, being one in spirit and purpose.*

Philippians 2:2

I passed the fresh vegetable aisle and rounded the corner to locate
brownie mix when my shopping cart collided into Melissa's. Laughingly, I greeted her, "Hey, Miss, great to run into you. Literally!
How's life with your man home again?" Melissa's husband had
returned a few weeks prior from his six-month Iraqi tour. I bubbled
with joy for her reunited family. The military base held a different energy the last few weeks, knowing that families of a deployed
squadron would soon be together.

When military personnel learn that a unit will return from an
overseas tour, the whole base buzzes with an unspoken excitement.
Home front spouses, whom I will refer to as "wingmen" (although
the majority are wing-women), commonly wait an entire year for

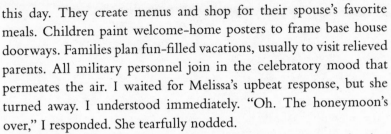

this day. They create menus and shop for their spouse's favorite meals. Children paint welcome-home posters to frame base house doorways. Families plan fun-filled vacations, usually to visit relieved parents. All military personnel join in the celebratory mood that permeates the air. I waited for Melissa's upbeat response, but she turned away. I understood immediately. "Oh. The honeymoon's over," I responded. She tearfully nodded.

Just as every wingman waits in great anticipation for her deployed soldier to return safely, she will attest to the challenging transition period (or reentry phase) that follows the joyful homecoming honeymoon. The first wave of transition rushes in after a soldier is deployed. In an eye's blink, wingmen assume the role of both parents: they fix plumbing leaks, shovel snow, stain decks, assemble Christmas trees, visit emergency rooms, undergo surgeries, cook holiday turkeys, mail graduation announcements, birth babies, and bury family members, and they accomplish these feats without their spouse. It's not a role for which they applied. No medals are awarded. Wingmen do these things because they must. They support their spouse's service to country and are honored to serve the same country by capably managing the home front. A wingman's inner strength, which is deeply seated in love, faith, and a passion for serving, allows a warrior to concentrate on the mission.

The second wave of transition gushes in like an unexpected tsunami. A few weeks after the welcome kisses dwindle and the last piece of homecoming cake is polished off, a role reversal suddenly occurs. Returning soldiers long to reclaim the captain's seat while wingmen are used to piloting the family jet solo. Wingmen have gained confidence and found that they possess the "right stuff" to handle the mission. These spouses never asked for wings, but once issued, it's difficult to hand them back. Returning soldiers often feel like strangers in their own homes.

One returning warrior swelled with pride, sharing how his wife expertly cared for their three children, the household, and her own thriving business while he served in Iraq, but his exuberance deflated as he confided how unneeded he felt after his return. In Iraq, he led a unit consisting of over two hundred soldiers who relied on his decisions daily. He shared that after the homecoming dust settled, he found himself remaining silent during discipline issues with his kids because his wife handled things differently and he did not want to interfere. He expressed that he felt like a background wall in his own home.

This transitional period is short-lived if couples learn to communicate their feelings early on. One wife advises wingmen to seek their spouses' advice on small matters, as well as the crucial ones, to help returning spouses feel needed. Avoid scheduling too many activities and provide family time together to talk. Returning warriors will regain their place within the family structure in time and the family dynamics will rebalance.

Not only do wingmen and warriors face transition challenges, but their kids do as well. Children are often more comfortable obeying wingmen and rebel against the returning parents' authority while transitioning back to a two-parent household. Children learn to manipulate their parents' emotions, and guilt and resentment slide their chairs up to the family table. The formerly absent parent feels

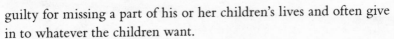

guilty for missing a part of his or her children's lives and often give in to whatever the children want.

Initially, returning soldiers may resent that their spouses reshaped household management methods while they were away. Returning warriors should realize that their wingmen have held down the fort for months. Even if the soldier would handle family situations differently if he or she manned the controls, there is no better fuel for the wingman's soul than appreciation. Remember, the wingman never asked to fly solo.

The worst mistake a returning soldier can make is to inform his or her spouse how badly situations were handled while he or she was deployed. Harsh words are spears to the heart and may cause irreversible damage. One returning soldier wisely advised, "You can't just add dad and stir. When you are gone, the family may be doing things differently to help them cope best. You can't walk in the door and change up the finances or jump right back into the disciplinarian role. You have to figure out what they are doing and jump in."

When my husband and I find ourselves at a disagreement crossroad, and I feel he is attacking my methods of discipline, finances, etc., there is one phrase he uses that gets me off the bench and back into the game. He reminds me, "Remember, we are on the same team." Immediately, my growing hurt or anger subsides. I know that we are both working for the same result, whether it is making the best decisions for our children, finances, or careers, or choosing what color to paint the kitchen. "Being on the same team" reminds me that God has joined us together in marriage to work together serving God for a common purpose.

When the external conflicts multiply, and they will, Tony and I have learned to reach out to God, knowing that we can triumph over any challenge when we rely on Him. When we join together and focus on our common goal, realizing we have different methods of reaching it, we fix our eyes on God and He helps us work harmoniously to get there.

Dear heavenly Father, thank you for blessing me with my spouse. Please help us unite in one spirit as we travel through life's transitions.

WHAT ARE THE BIGGEST CHALLENGES you face during military transitions? How do you readjust after being separated? How can you reassure your spouse that you are on the same team? What goals do you share? Do you have different ideas of how to achieve them? Have you both brought your challenges to God?

Resources

Military Family Network's Emilitary.org is the military candy store for website links pertaining to every aspect of family life. They offer a great relocation guide for before, during, and after moves. Afterdeployment.com is a wellness resource for the military community. Their mission is to help service members, their families, and veterans overcome common adjustment problems following a deployment. Military Homefront's site has many resources that can help military members, spouses, and families cope with the challenges and thrive during deployment or reserve mobilization. Military One Source offers a helpful site on family transitions after deployment. Search for the web page, "Returning to Family Life After Deployment." The National Center for PTSD provides a wonderful family video regarding family transitioning. Search the site for "Returning from the War Zone: A Guide for Families of Military Personnel" and the "Family and Friends Fact Sheet." Learn more about these organizations and websites in the Resources section in the back of this book.

PART 3

Loneliness and Grief

FOURTEEN

A New Day's Dawn

Finding Hope after Loss

I tell you the truth, if you have faith as small as a mustard seed, you can say to this mountain, "Move from here to there" and it will move. Nothing will be impossible for you.

Matthew 17:20

Captain Michael Dodson leaned across the faded seat of his beloved old white pickup truck and tenderly squeezed his wife's hand as they began their drive to Barksdale Air Force Base in Louisiana. Good-byes never got easier, but Mike couldn't help but smile, thinking how blessed he was. Mike's passion for his wife, Cheryl, outranked everything, even flying the B-52 bomber—his second love.

When Mike returned from his four-month deployment to Guam, he and Cheryl would start a family. They were the poster couple for responsible family planning. They saved up a nest egg, paid off bills, bought baby furniture and clothes, and even decided on a Noah's ark theme for the baby's room. Everything was in place—except the baby, but that would certainly change once Cheryl resigned her RN position at the hospital to stay at home.

Mike and Cheryl savored the ten-minute ride like the last bite of a favorite dinner before a surgical operation, knowing the bland, restricted diet that would soon follow. They drove alongside the familiar railroad tracks leading to the base. Cheryl reassured herself, "In just four months, he will be home." In fact, she surprised Mike with an engraved St. Christopher's medal, which read, "I'll see you when you get home."

The weeks lingered on. Mike's calls from Guam always lifted Cheryl's spirits. Before hanging up, Mike declared rather than asked, "Do you know how much I love you!" Cheryl embraced the warmth of Mike's words; he usually showed his love through actions. Cheryl recalled the day when Mike returned from work, laid out her favorite outfit to wear, drove her to a rented plane, and flew her to a quaint diner in the middle of nowhere that he discovered in a travel book. The evening played out like a Hollywood movie, but Cheryl was not acting. Her life was *real*. Mike rarely declared his devotion through "I love yous," but for some reason, before his July 21 mission, he did, and the words warmed Cheryl's heart.

That same day on another continent, Colonel George Martin, to his wife's delight, planned the cookout himself, surprising his beautiful Samoan bride of eight years. Ursula *always* organized get-togethers with the Laanans, who were as close as friends could get to family without sharing DNA. As he grilled, George jokingly boasted about his two favorite foods: his famous London broil and the tasty barbecue ribs prepared by their dear friend, Mom Rose. He excitedly talked to his nephew DJ about flying the B-52 the following day during Guam's Liberation Day parade.

Colonel Martin, the 36th Medical Group Commander and flight surgeon at Andersen Air Force Base in Guam, set a sky-scraping standard for colleagues to follow due to his skill, professionalism, and respect for others. Not only did his career soar, but in just one month, George would embrace his newborn miracle baby. Ursula's unexpected pregnancy blessed them after seven years of trying, coupled with an arduous process of infertility procedures. Ursula finally succumbed to researching adoption agencies when she discovered the fantastic news. *God was good.*

George lovingly gazed across the deck at Ursula. He adored his independent wife who he nicknamed TC ("Tough Chick"). She nurtured everyone around her. Never a tear. Never a complaint. Tough as Kevlar on the outside, Ursula allowed no one to take care of her—no one but George. He knew her inside-out and wanted to give her the world. In turn, she ignited his passion for life. As George breathed in Guam's gentle tropical breeze, he realized that life didn't get any better than that moment. After the meal, George pulled away from the Laanans' home while shouting from the open car window, "Tomorrow, I will be waving to you from the sky!"

At 1:30 a.m. and 12:00 p.m. on two continents, two women, Ursula and Cheryl, opened their doors to a military leader and a friend who informed them that Raider 21 had gone down, their husbands were aboard, and that a skilled rescue team was searching for survivors. Two women dropped to their knees on different sides of the world, uniting in the same prayer for inner strength and hope that their husbands survived—but that was not to be. On July 21, 2008, two patriotic military wives became widows overnight.

After the last note of taps sounded and the flags were folded, two commonalities linked these women together and pulled them through the toughest time of their lives: strength from their faith in God and love from friends and family. Cheryl and Ursula agreed that no words needed to be spoken. Just a friend's presence meant he or she cared. Their lawns were mowed and their houses cleaned. Their individual squadron spouses cooked and catered breakfast, lunch, and dinner daily for weeks. Cheryl's hospital cafeteria cooked meals also. The women agreed that loved ones reminiscing about their husbands gave comfort. Cheryl confided, as Ursula nodded, "Some people avoided speaking about our husbands in efforts to sidestep pain, but that was more hurtful. Their memories keep them alive in our hearts." She added, "The best advice offered were the simple words, 'You will smile again one day.' I clung to that hope."

Ursula leaned on Job 1:21–22 for strength and understanding: "Naked came I out of my mother's womb, and naked shall I return thither: the LORD gave, and the LORD hath taken away; blessed be the name of the Lord. In all this Job sinned not, nor charged God foolishly" (KJV). Many people shy from these difficult verses, but God blessed Ursula with unique insight and determined hope. She said,

> My husband left and took nothing with him. I looked at all of his belongings and literally said to myself, we really take nothing with us when our time comes.

There I was—alone in our home with all of his earthly possessions . . . but I knew George would be upset if I drowned in self-pity, so I focused on my blessings and how fortunate I was having George in my life for that time. I knew that I was loved deeply, a love that many people never experience in a lifetime. I thank God for him. All I am and have is from God. The story of Job strengthened me, for the Lord knew Job could and would endure all that Satan would do. I wanted to prove myself worthy of the blessings that I was able to enjoy.

After Cheryl read, "I tell you the truth, if you have faith as small as a mustard seed, you can say to this mountain, 'Move from here to there' and it will move. Nothing will be impossible for you" (Matthew 17:20), she drove to the market. Cheryl wanted to visualize how small her faith could be for God to still work in her life. "I put mustard seeds on a piece of Scotch tape. I carried some in my wallet and attached the others to my bathroom mirror so I could see them every day. I stood in front of that mirror each morning and looked at the mustard seeds as a reminder that if I had just a smidgeon of faith, like the tiny seed, I could make it through the day." And she did. Cheryl not only braved that day, but nearly two years later she and Ursula speak on behalf of Tragedy Assistance Programs for Survivors (TAPS). TAPS offers immediate and long-term emotional help, hope, and healing to anyone grieving the death of a loved one in military service, regardless of his or her relationship to the deceased or the circumstances of the death. This organization supports survivors through a network of peer mentors. Cheryl said, "One of the hardest things is that you are no longer a spouse. You are not a retiree. You are just a death beneficiary." Ursula added, "When we walked into the TAPS conference room, we were surrounded by strength. You have immediate connections. Every member is a survivor. Every mentor is a trained volunteer who has lost a military loved one. You are paired up with other survivors as best as possible, according to their branch of service, similar rank, and similar circumstance."

Although complete strangers when Raider 21 went down off Guam's coast, Ursula and Cheryl became best friends the moment they met. Knowing their husbands were together during their last moments bonded them spiritually. They draw insurmountable strength from each other's friendship. A meaningful moment reaffirmed this connection after they stepped onto the original rescue boat two months after the accident. When the ship neared the exact crash site coordinates, two white doves flew above the ship from seemingly nowhere. The crew had never seen doves so far from shore before. The graceful birds united and hovered together right above Ursula and Cheryl, and then separated and soared away. The women reflected on this moment, "The doves signify to us hope and peace. We felt Michael and George's presence . . . like the two of them were assuring the two of us that they were together and okay and that we would be okay too."

Lord, bless the families of fallen soldiers. Surround them with your loving arms. Lead them to encouraging friends and helpful counsel, and assure them that you steadfastly hold their hand.

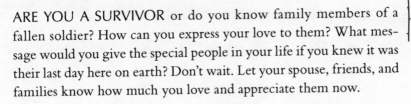

ARE YOU A SURVIVOR or do you know family members of a fallen soldier? How can you express your love to them? What message would you give the special people in your life if you knew it was their last day here on earth? Don't wait. Let your spouse, friends, and families know how much you love and appreciate them now.

Resource

For more information about assisting survivors of military tragedies or distributing TAPS information to a military base, visit taps .org or call 800-959-TAPS (8277).

The Road Back Home

Winning Battles in the Post-Traumatic Stress Disorder War

A cord of three strands is not quickly broken.

Ecclesiastes 4:12

Independent Medical Duty Technician Sergeant Shane Lacaillade worked with the US Army as an emergency management advisor to the Iraqi Army.[11] His position was equivalent to a civilian Federal Emergency Management Agency (FEMA) director and a physician's assistant. Shane linked Iraqi soldiers and civilians to American medical care via medevac.[12] Sergeant Lacaillade evaluated every scenario, from appendicitis to mutilated body limbs, for possible medevac transport. A patient's life or death often depended on Shane's judgment call—denying medevac transport meant the wounded were

---

11. Sergeant Shane Lacaillade's story is used by permission.
12. Medevac is the system that transports the wounded to medical facilities using helicopters.

forced back onto the same IED[13] and sniper-infested road where the injuries first occurred.

At 6:00 p.m., the workday wound down at the small Iraqi military training base known as Kirkush, just ten miles from the Iranian border. Sergeant Lacaillade ignored the 110-degree temperature, threw on his workout clothes, and prepared to lift weights with a friend when the phone rang. A suicide bombing required his clinic's urgent assistance. A female terrorist, posing as a pregnant woman, had slipped into an Iraqi wedding reception unnoticed and detonated her hidden vest bomb, turning the couple's happy day into a bloody massacre. To make matters worse, a second bomb, timed precisely to the rescue team's arrival, had detonated, creating a second wave of wounded civilians.

Three severely injured adult males arrived first through the clinic's doors. Sergeant Lacaillade quickly tended to one of the patients as two Iraqi doctors initiated care for the others. Just as Shane's patient stabilized, he heard the clinic's doors fly open and loud Arabic screaming. Bloodstained civilians carried in three limp bodies. One Iraqi doctor, unable to handle the chaos, walked outside for air and never returned. Shane phoned his military brothers: a missile commander, service members, and heating and ventilating technicians—not one recruit had a medical background, but Shane had no other options. As Shane applied tourniquets above the limbs that doctors amputated without morphine, the doors flew open again with more yelling and more patients.

---

13. IEDs are improvised explosive devices, or homemade roadside bombs that are detonated in a variety of ways, from cell phones to trip wires on Christmas tree lights.

When Shane walked to a reserved room to verify the wounds of those not expected to survive, he heard whimpering similar to a puppy's. He poked his head in the back room and discovered two baby girls, approximately ten and eighteen months old. Their bloodied faces and abdomens were laced with shrapnel. Since the Iraqi culture values men over women and children, the Iraqis had placed the girls in the reserved area and drew the curtain, hiding their presence. Shane's concern elevated when he noticed they weren't crying—a dangerous sign. Thoughts raced back to his family and three children in America. Shane immediately refocused his efforts on the girls while he shouted triage orders to his newly recruited comrades.

Thirty-one of the sixty-five people injured in the brutal attack were sent to Sergeant Lacaillade's small, undermanned clinic, where five patients died. In two grueling hours, Shane had prioritized the remaining wounded for a large-scale transport by Blackhawk helicopters or ground evacuation to various trauma centers while simultaneously providing hands-on medical care.

After the crisis, the pressure cooker of accumulating emotions took its toll on Sergeant Lacaillade and his unit. One soldier became so aggressive that he was transferred to Germany. There he received post-traumatic stress disorder (PTSD) treatment. PTSD is an anxiety disorder induced by experiencing or witnessing a traumatic event. The afflicted person recalls the event's trauma as if it were currently happening. Symptoms may include—but are not limited to—emotional numbing, sleep problems, flashbacks, irritability, hypervigilance, depression, anxiety, isolation, and poor concentration or memory.

Symptoms usually appear within the first three months of the traumatic event, but may be delayed for years. For a diagnosis, two or more symptoms must last more than thirty days and cause significant distress or impairment of daily life. One can have all the symptoms, but if they're not disrupting daily life activities, then the person is diagnosed with post-traumatic stress, but not the disorder.

Sergeant Lacaillade noticed changes in himself. His once happy-go-lucky demeanor was now hypervigilant and suspecting. He angered easily. He questioned why God allowed the challenging work conditions he experienced to continue. Shane feared that if he sought counsel, he would appear weak to his troops, since he was everyone's go-to man; therefore, Shane pocketed the stress during his entire one-year tour.

Shane eventually returned home to Missouri. He said of his return home, "The first night home my family and I went to eat at a busy restaurant. Loud noise really bothered me. There were too many people. The noise reminded me of the convoys. I had to get out. I didn't even tell my family that I was leaving. I just left." Shane's seventeen-year-old daughter, Brenna, shared that her father's driving took on a new definition: "No one wanted to get in the car with dad. He would speed and dodge potholes like they were road bombs. When we approached stop signs, he would sit there and scan the entire area like he was looking for snipers." Shane nearly got into an accident three times when crossing the city's overpass while a train's horn blared below. "My first reaction was to hit the brakes, turn, and duck. Everyone in the car would scream, 'Dad, what are you doing?'" Shane knew these unhealthy reactions were harmful.

On Shane's second tour to Iraq, he found counsel from a wonderful military chaplain, Major Fitzgerald (better known to his troops as "Chappy"). Like many chaplains selflessly serving in combat, this man of God routinely looked into the eyes of young airman, soldiers, sailors, and marines who are drowning in a sea of despair and doubts and shared with them what applies to all soldiers: "You are infinitely important to God—and to many others. So don't let these days of darkness take away who you truly are. In Christ, we are victorious. All of life is TDY, merely temporary duty. Our permanent place of station is with God eternally. But while we are here, we are called to make a difference in the battle against evil and injustice." Routine visits to the inspiring chaplain helped rebuild Shane's faith, and Shane was baptized.

Shane's outlook improved. He learned to confide his fears to a good friend and worked out twice a day. He now urges soldiers to find an outlet for bottled stress: "Military is a brotherhood. Don't fall into the pressure cooker syndrome. You become dangerous to yourselves and others. If the first person with whom you try to communicate doesn't respond, find another person until someone listens. There are usually chaplains at every FOB[14] and medical clinic."

At first, Shane thought receiving counseling gave him a stigma, and he didn't want to upset his family by sharing his experiences, but he now realizes his strength comes from God. His message to

---

14. FOB is a forward operating base, which is "an airfield used to support tactical operations without establishing full support facilities" (US Department of Defense, *The Dictionary of Military Terms* [New York: Skyhorse Publishing, 2009], 217).

military members is, "You're not the only one going through this. You're not alone."

Navy Chaplain Daniel Roysden stated in an interview, "Finding someone to accept their story without being afraid that it will traumatize them is crucial for healthy well being."[15] Roysden has counseled numerous returning soldiers from Iraq and Afghanistan at Fallon Naval Station, Nevada. Many of these soldiers participated in black operations, which is a special force comprised of highly trained, brave individuals that often pave the way for following troops to better complete their mission. Roysden shared that numerous soldiers avoided his office for fear that receiving counsel carried a stigma; however, if he shared lunch with an individual, met someone in a doctor's office, or even shared a Wal-Mart checkout line with a returning soldier, emotions freely flowed.

In an interview with Lindy Williamson, a trauma expert and ICISF[16] instructor, she reaffirmed that people undergoing severe traumatic experiences prefer talking with others who have also witnessed similar trauma. She added that those with PTSD are also helped by a combination of physical fitness, volunteering, and education about PTSD for themselves, family, and friends. She recommends committing to a thirty-day exercise program that stresses a state of relaxation of both body and mind, such as tai chi or yoga.

---

15. Chaplain Daniel Roysden's remarks, given in an interview on May 27, 2010, are used by permission.

16. ICISF is the International Critical Incident Stress Foundation, "a nonprofit foundation dedicated to the prevention and mitigation of disabling stress through the provision of education, training, and support services for varied organizations and communities worldwide." See http://www.icisf.org/.

These exercise programs also help with sleep disorders—another challenge common to war veterans. Helping others by volunteering reestablishes a sense of meaningful purpose. By educating themselves about PTSD and receiving counsel from empathetic people, veterans take ownership of their challenges at their own pace, regain a stronger sense of self, and begin to heal.[17]

Recovery occurs with help from others. In aviation, flying in formation provides strength. Wingmen alert fellow wingmen to threats, such as thunderstorms or enemy aircraft. If one wingman fails to maintain position due to maintenance or psychological problems, the formation compensates for the weaker partner until the issue is resolved. If a wingman's instruments malfunction, he watches the wing of another aircraft until he's safely guided to the ground. The words from the classic hit movie *Top Gun* ring true: "You *never, never* leave your wingman!"

As wingmen, we encourage and guide distressed warriors back into formation, and one of the most effective ways to do that is by listening to them. Sergeant Shane Lacaillade says, "If you are the person someone is confiding in, put aside whatever you are doing and lend an ear. You might save someone from going over the edge." If someone shares with you his or her thoughts of suicide, then getting that person professional help is urgent. Most people share their decision to end their life prior to carrying it out. Trained professionals, including chaplains, medics, and counselors, can help figure out the experiences that caused PTSD. The wingmen's ultimate purpose

17. Lindy Williamson's advice, given in an interview on May 30, 2010, is used by permission.

is to accomplish the formation's mission safely. During every flight, unforeseen challenges arise, but there is strength in numbers.

Learning from prior warriors' experiences can spare future warriors from PTSD and related depression. Educate yourself, family, and friends about PTSD before, during, and after deployments. Visit the websites listed below and in the back of the book for numerous helpful resources. Talk with others who have witnessed similar traumatic episodes. Use your wingmen—seek out fellow Christian warriors and pray with them regularly. Utilize counselors, chaplains, and professional services, such as militaryonesource.com. Find a good friend to confide in. Exercise, and find a worthy cause to volunteer your time and energy. Finally, and most importantly, ask God, the *ultimate* wingman, to guide and protect your formation.

The road back home presents challenges. The war of PTSD is real, but if the guidelines offered are implemented, individual battles can be won, relationships can grow stronger, and fulfilling lives can be lived. God awaits your call so that He can share your sufferings and give you strength. One of my favorite Bible stories is that of Peter and Jesus walking on the water (see Matthew 14:25–33). When Peter takes his eyes off Jesus and is distracted by the surrounding storm, he begins to lose faith and drown. But when Peter calls out to Jesus, he is rescued by Christ's hand, and God can do the same for you if you call out to Him.

Lord, thank you for unveiling your strength when I feel out of control. Help me to surrender my anxieties to you. Lead me to encouraging friends who will strengthen my faith. Reveal your presence to me when I face tough circumstances, and give me wisdom and discernment to listen to my fellow man during their times of distress. Help me find the peace that comes through knowing you.

ARE TORMENTING SCENARIOS lingering in your mind and robbing you of sleep or interfering with your daily activities? Do you ever feel out of control? Do you pray with a friend and confide your fears? Have you brought your concerns to the Lord? Have you thought about seeking professional counsel?

Resources

Help is available for combat veterans who have experienced post-traumatic stress disorder, traumatic brain injury, or both. The following organizations and websites expertly address these issues. Learn more about them in the Resources section in the back of this book.

- Both the American Legion and the Veterans of Foreign Warfare (VFW) are worthy organizations comprised of veterans helping other veterans, their families, and communities.
- Adopt a Chaplain is a Christ-centered ministry, the only national charity that exclusively serves deployed chaplains.
- Called to Serve Ministry is a military support site that discusses PTSD-related topics. The "R & R Room" offers encouragement, hope, and support through inspirational stories and related Scripture. On the site, spouses and warriors experiencing similar

situations can encourage and pray for one another, and find helpful links to additional resources.

- Combat Faith provides Christian encouragement and education for military members wishing to strengthen their faith in God and veterans challenged with serious issues related to relationship struggles, substance abuse, and PTSD.

- *Day of Discovery*'s "The War Within: Finding Hope for Post-Traumatic Stress" is a four-part video series where veterans and their loved ones whose lives have been drastically changed by war will find encouragement.

- The Department of Defense established a twenty-four-hour, toll-free hotline number, (866) 966-1020, and two websites to help with PTSD and military-related challenges. Afterdeployment.org provides self-care solutions targeting post-traumatic stress, depression, and other behavioral health challenges commonly faced after a deployment through self-assessments and media-rich resources. Realwarriors.net was launched by the Defense Centers of Excellence for Psychological Health and Traumatic Brain Injury to promote the processes of building resilience, facilitating recovery, and supporting reintegration of returning service members, veterans, and their families.

- *Family of a Vet* gives advice on how to cope, survive, and thrive the "aftershocks" of combat including PTSD and Traumatic Brain Injury (TBI). This difficult subject matter is explained in easy layman's terms.

- Hopefortheheroes.com provides Christian help for PTSD. Daily messages of hope are delivered by phone, text, or e-mail.
- International Critical Incident Stress Foundation (ICISF) is a non-profit foundation dedicated to the prevention and mitigation of disabling stress. ICISF provides leadership, education, training, consultation, and support services in crisis intervention and disaster behavioral health services to the emergency response professions, other organizations, and communities worldwide.
- Militaryministry.org serves military members, veterans, and families through direct ministry and partnerships with chaplains, churches, and organizations. This organization offers military marriage seminars; chaplain retreats; "bridges to healing" for returning warriors, veterans, and their families; and When War Comes Home retreats for spouses of combat veterans affected by PTSD.
- Military OneSource is a 24/7 resource that also offers three kinds of short-term, non-medical counseling options to active duty, guard, and reserve members and their families. The website, militaryonesource.com, provides confidential counseling online.
- The National Center for Post-Traumatic Stress Disorder, Department of Veterans Affairs, addresses the needs of veterans with military-related PTSD.
- NotAlone.com is a resource center and meeting room where warriors and spouses can confidentially meet online with other

veterans and families for counseling and to discuss PTSD and other related topics with fellow veterans and family members.

- Operation Homefront, Wounded Warrior Wives. Through on-site support communities, and a virtual community that includes an online discussion forum, Wounded Warrior Wives provides female caregivers with opportunities to build relationships, access resources, and enjoy brief moments of rest and respite from their care-giving responsibilities.

- Point Man International Ministries connects the hurting veteran, as well as their families and friends, with others who have already begun the transition home after war.

- *Finding My Way: A Teen's Guide to Living with a Parent Who Has Experienced Trauma* by Michelle D. Sherman and DeAnne Sherman (Minneapolis: Beavers Pond Press, 2006) is an interactive workbook used by a number of military families and behavioral health specialists to help teens cope with having a parent who has experienced trauma.

- War experiences and reaction to combat stress can lead depressed people to think about hurting or even killing themselves. If you think you or your family member may be feeling suicidal, contact the National Suicide Prevention Lifeline at 800-273-TALK (8255) or visit www.suicidepreventionlifeline.org.

SIXTEEN

Will He Ever Really Come Home?

Restoring Hope to Families Living with Post-Traumatic Stress Disorder

For the battle is not yours, but God's.

2 Chronicles 20:15

"What do you want?" the angry voice shouted from the other side of the bathroom door in response to the gentle knock. Seven-year-old Brody fearfully replied as if he were confessing to breaking a window, "Mom just wanted to know if you wanted pancakes for breakfast." Brody ran to the kitchen without waiting for his dad's reply and blurted out, "I liked daddy lots better before he went away." Faith sighed, "I know how you feel, honey, but we have to remember to be patient. It's only been three months since daddy came home from Afghanistan. It's going to take a while."

Faith had prepared herself for homecoming changes by attending base briefings on family deployment transitions but, like her son, she still wanted life to reset to pre-deployment "normal." The laid-back Jerry that Faith knew cracked jokes and counted down the days until April 1 so that he could pull pranks on family and friends. The returning Jerry rarely even smiled. In response to minor frustrations, he punched walls, and then became confused seeing the broken plaster thirty minutes later, not recalling how it happened. When he wasn't working at the base, he only played video games or watched TV and slept, and nightmares plagued his once restful sleep. He would awaken, startled, and drenched in sweat. At night Jerry flinched whenever Faith touched him. She felt rejected and wondered if he still loved her.

The last public function she and Jerry attended was a graduation two months earlier. When a folding chair collapsed and the loud "bang" ricocheted through the gymnasium, Jerry ducked under the bleachers as if he were under enemy attack, and then fled from the ceremony. Faith explained to her friends that Jerry's quick exit was work related, which was truer than anyone realized. Later when Faith encouraged Jerry to go to counseling, he stormed from the room. The man who previously couldn't wait to come home from work to share his day, shoot hoops with his kids, wow friends with his barbecuing finesse, and cuddle with his wife while watching a movie deployed fifteen months ago. Although Jerry was in the next room, she feared he would never really come home.

Stories like Faith's are all too common since researchers believe up to one-third of returning combat veterans exhibit symptoms of post-traumatic stress syndrome (PTSD), traumatic brain injury

(TBI),[18] or major depression.[19] A spouse who lives with a combat warrior's unpredictable behaviors is often experiencing secondary post-traumatic stress disorder, also known as secondary traumatic stress (STS) and compassion fatigue. A spouse with STS mirrors the symptoms of the warrior. Once a spouse identifies the triggers, or cues that precipitate PTSD symptoms in her warrior (i.e., loud noises, the smell of fuel, litter on the road), she walks on eggshells, anticipating an emotional meltdown to happen. She becomes hyper-vigilant, much like the deployed warrior who constantly surveys the road while driving, searching for destructive IEDs. This protective method is used by both the warrior and the spouse in order to avoid triggers and diffuse stressful situations. Spouses may isolate themselves from friends, become lonely, and feel depressed. They grieve the loss of the spouse they loved and married even though they are thankful their warrior survived. Jenny Andrews, who counsels warriors and family members, stated in an interview, "Spouses of combat veterans tend to minimize their trauma, thinking that their stress is nothing compared to the 'bad stuff' their warrior went through, so they don't believe that they deserve STS counseling treatment. Nothing could be farther from the truth."[20]

18. According to the Brain Injury Association of America, traumatic brain injury is a blow or jolt to the head or a penetrating head injury that disrupts the function of the brain. See biausa.org.
19. Terri Tanielian, Lisa H. Jaycox, Terry L. Schell, Grant N. Marshall, M. Audrey Burnam, Christine Eibner, Benjamin R. Karney, Lisa S. Meredith, Jeanne S. Ringel, and Mary E. Vaiana, *Invisible Wounds of War: Summary and Recommendations for Addressing Psychological and Cognitive Injuries* (Santa Monica, CA: RAND Corporation, 2008), available at http://www.rand.org/pubs/monographs/MG720z1.
20. Interview conducted on January 5, 2011.

Before warriors come home, spouses experience a gamut of stressors that predispose them to STS. Oftentimes they spend up to a year fearing that their warriors may not return home safely. After combat veterans do return, spouses experience an exhilarating homecoming high—but not for long. Despair follows when spouses of warriors battling PTSD wonder if their lives will ever return to normal. Since many warriors cannot assume their prior household responsibilities, at least initially, the home-front spouse continues to assume duties such as finances, house upkeep, and child care. The warrior's physical or mental disabilities may force a stay-at-home mom into the workforce to compensate for the loss of income, creating guilt and resentment in the mom for leaving small children. Further, more stress is loaded on when home-front spouses become the glue that hold relationships between warriors and immediate and extended families together.

What can spouses do to treat STS? Andrews said, "Every warrior, spouse, and family member should educate themselves by reading everything they can get their hands on about PTSD." She stressed how important it is for the home-front spouse to safeguard her mental and physical health before she can care for her family. Indulging in fulfilling hobbies, exercising, and interacting socially helps reduce stress. Sharing experiences with fellow spouses undergoing similar circumstances is therapeutic. Don't try to heal the invisible wounds inflicted by combat trauma yourself.

Marshele Waddell, author of *Hope for the Home Front* and *When War Comes Home*, met PTSD when her Navy Seal husband returned from Iraq as a stranger. She writes,

I took some important steps toward healing for myself and on behalf of my husband and children: I went to God. More frequently on my face than on my knees, I called on the Lord. I relied on my Savior to intercede for me and on his Holy Spirit to pray for me when I couldn't find the words. While my human tendency in my pain was to pull away from God and other believers, I committed to guarding my one-on-one times with God and to continue to worship and fellowship with his family—come what may.[21]

After Marshele sought God's strength, she called on Christian sisters who would earnestly pray for her, connected with Military Ministry of Campus Crusade for Christ, and asked her church leadership to refer her to a licensed Christian female counselor skilled in working with military families. Marshele's husband refused to go to counseling, so for two years, she attended counseling alone. As a result, Marshele and her husband began to make progress as a couple. They have learned to more quickly recognize the symptom's triggers and more effectively communicate with one another.

All professionals skilled in treating combat stress–related injuries agree that counseling is an invaluable weapon against PTSD symptoms. Spouses are encouraged not to push their warriors or demand they attend counseling. Combat veterans shun counseling for two reasons: They fear that seeking help will affect their command because counseling is considered a sign of weakness (in their

---

21. Marshele Carter Waddell, "The War at Home," *Today's Christian Woman*, 2007.

mind, counseling is affirmation that they are going crazy); and veterans feel they are alone in their battle with PTSD.

Spouses are more successful convincing their warrior to join counseling by undergoing a *you*-ectomy. For instance, if Faith said, "Jerry, *you* need help. *Your* crazy behaviors are tearing us apart. *You* need counseling, or our marriage may not last," Jerry would feel attacked, believing Faith thinks he is crazy. In turn, he would build a wall against the professional help he needs. Removing "you" from the vocabulary eliminates blaming Jerry for lack of emotional control. Spouses who successfully initiate counseling approach their warriors saying, "*I'd* like to go to counseling so *I* can better understand the challenges *we* are going through so *we* can get through this *together*." Convincing Jerry that his behaviors are normal reactions to an abnormal situation assures him that he's not going crazy. If warriors still refuse to attend counseling, spouses are advised to go alone. Once veterans witness positive changes, they may be more inclined to attend themselves.

The following lists were compiled after interviewing numerous spouses and PTSD professionals about helpful PTSD coping techniques.

What You Can Do for Your Warrior

- Self-educate about PTSD before, during, and after deployments so both the spouse and warrior can identify symptoms and seek treatment immediately if they occur.
- Pray before choosing a counselor. Make sure your counselor is *experienced* in treating trauma, committed for the "long haul,"

and willing to educate the family about PTSD. Avoid counselors advocating drug therapy and in lieu of counseling.

- Steer warriors back to hobbies they previously enjoyed before deploying. By reconnecting to prior interests instead of initiating new activities, warriors return to familiar, comfortable places that divert stress and are fulfilling.

- Identify triggers by keeping a daily journal. For instance, if a warrior periodically has a panic attack, a daily journal may reveal that dinners with rice triggered traumatic memories. The warrior recalls an IED exploding, taking the life of his comrade—just after eating a meal containing rice.

- Create a special word or hand signal to avert emotional outbursts, alerting each other when anger is brewing. Then take a time-out and reconvene at a *designated* time to discuss the issue when emotions calm.

- Order a Chill Drill device, available through the DOD's Military OneSource. This audio resource resembles an iPod and transmits a relaxation exercise from a trained therapist to discretely calm potentially traumatic situations triggered by noisy, crowded areas. Another option is to carry an mp3 player loaded with the warrior's favorite music to drone out loud, stress-triggering noise.

- Never awaken a warrior while he is sleeping. Several spouses recalled waking their warriors from nightmares and then being choked or hit because the warriors were confused, thinking they were under attack. If this occurs, seek immediate counsel, and sleep in separate rooms. (One spouse learned to toss an

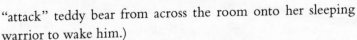

"attack" teddy bear from across the room onto her sleeping warrior to wake him.)

- Keep a prayer diary and read your prayers to each other daily, and share Scripture together—it is a powerful tool to strengthen relationships between each other and God.

- Don't push warriors to be "like they were before" because that won't happen. Get to know the "new" person and grow your relationship together.

What You Can Do for Yourself

- *Never* remain in a threatening environment. Protect children and self first. After the crisis passes, help the warrior understand that protecting the family is necessary, but leaving a dangerous situation is *not* equivalent to giving up on the relationship. Communicate that the warrior is wanted in your life but *needs* to get healthy for the family.

- Know that you are not responsible for your warrior's behavior. Undesirable behavior due to combat stress is a normal reaction to an abnormal event. Memorize this. Write it on your forehead if needed.

- Give yourself permission not to be perfect. If the house collects clutter and the kids' hair looks like a tornado landed on their heads, ease up on yourself and concentrate on your accomplishments.

- Plan to attend a When War Comes Home retreat presented by Hope for the Homefront and Military Ministry to help you with every aspect of PTSD and combat trauma. See the Resources section in the back of this book for more information.

- Join an online military forum and connect with spouses experiencing PTSD-related challenges.
- Find an older mentor who has walked in your shoes. Mentors can give you insight as to what to expect in the future.
- Exercise regularly. Join the base fitness center and attend a variety of stress-relieving, calorie-burning classes.
- Give yourself permission to grieve. Find time to get away from your home, spouse, and children to have a good cry. Visit your base chaplain and share your grief.
- Memorize Scripture for daily doses of spiritual strength.

What You Can Do as a Family

- Encourage volunteerism. This can be a family activity that promotes a sense of purpose (which is oftentimes lost after experiencing combat trauma).
- Keep a family journal in a central location. Potentially bottled emotions become free once they are jotted down. A family journal allows warriors and family members to process situations, choose words wisely, and think about solutions before confronting a family member one-on-one.
- Avoid crowded, noisy events, especially after a warrior returns and has not had time to adjust.
- Spend time with your children. PTSD is confusing, especially to children who may think they are causing the warrior's behaviors. Even though you reassure them that PTSD is no

one's fault, they may still feel responsible. Initiate counseling immediately for them.

- Attend family counseling even if the warrior is not currently symptomatic. Make sure the counselor is *experienced* in treating trauma and willing to educate the family on the possibility of delayed symptoms, which can appear months to years after the trauma occurred.
- Pray together, read the Scriptures, and go to church. God honors and blesses those who diligently seek Him.

PTSD is a lifelong war, but understanding the causes and symptoms is key to winning daily battles. With the proper guidance, tools, and strength that comes from seeking God, victory can be yours.

The unexpected kiss on Faith's neck caused her to spin around, dropping her spatula on the wooden floor. Laughingly she said, "Jerry, knock that off. You scared me to death!" Fourteen months had now passed since Jerry's return from combat. Faith entered into counseling after Jerry's onset of PTSD symptoms. Jerry joined her four months later. Together they invested their free time to understand PTSD—and not just how to survive, but how to grow stronger because of it. Faith attended an inspirational retreat and gained a better understanding of STS. They both talk regularly to veterans and spouses who have been touched by PTSD. Although she and Jerry know that PTSD doesn't disappear, they no longer fear losing their future together. They memorized Psalm 145:13–14: "The LORD is faithful to all his promises and loving toward all he has made. The LORD upholds all those who fall and lifts up all who are bowed down." Only God could lift them up and restore hope. Faith returned Jerry's embrace, and he softly whispered in her ear, "It's good to be home."

Dear Lord, please help heal those hurting from the invisible wounds of combat. Renew their spirit, restore their severed relationships, and let them find rest in you.

WHAT STEPS HAVE YOU TAKEN before a deployment to learn about the effects of PTSD? If you haven't taken any, it's not too late. If you or someone you know has been touched by the aftershock of combat, numerous resources listed below offer military and spiritual support.

Resources

Learn more about the following organizations and websites in the Resources section in the back of this book.

- Combat Faith provides Christian encouragement and education for military members wishing to strengthen their faith in God and veterans challenged with serious issues related to relationship struggles, substance abuse, and PTSD.
- Called to Serve Ministry is a refuge for spouses to openly and confidentially discuss military challenges, including PTSD and secondary PTSD. Numerous resources and helpful links fill the support page. Limited scholarships for When War Comes Home retreats are available at this site.

- *Family of a Vet* gives advice on how to cope, survive, and thrive the "aftershocks" of combat including PTSD and Traumatic Brain Injury (TBI). This difficult subject matter is explained in easy layman's terms.

- Militaryministry.org serves military members, veterans, and families through direct ministry and partnerships with chaplains, churches, and organizations. This organization offers military marriage seminars; chaplain retreats; "bridges to healing" for returning warriors, veterans, and their families; and When War Comes Home retreats for spouses of combat veterans affected by PTSD.

- NotAlone.com is a resource center and meeting room where warriors and spouses can confidentially meet online with other veterans and families for counseling and to discuss PTSD and other related topics with fellow veterans and family members.

- Operation Homefront, Wounded Warrior Wives. Through on-site support communities, and a virtual community that includes an online discussion forum, Wounded Warrior Wives provides female caregivers with opportunities to build relationships, access resources, and enjoy brief moments of rest and respite from their care-giving responsibilities.

- Point Man International Ministries connects the hurting veteran, as well as their families and friends, with others who have already begun the transition home after war. The organization states, "With Jesus Christ as our focal point, it is our desire to provide spiritual and emotional healing."

- The Real Warriors campaign is an initiative launched by the Defense Centers of Excellence (DCoE) for Psychological Health and Traumatic Brain Injury to promote the processes of building resilience, facilitating recovery, and supporting reintegration of returning service members, veterans, and their families.
- Vietnam Veteran Wives reaches out to veterans and their spouses and families. The website addresses benefits for spouses and children, Veterans Administration claims, PTSD issues, Dependency and Indemnity Compensation (DIC) claims, and benefits after service. VVW is available to all veterans' wives and contains real-life stories of pain and hope.
- When War Comes Home retreats are weekend experiences for women touched by the lives and service of combat veterans of any conflict. Everything regarding PTSD is available at this conference, the most important being hope.
- *When War Comes Home: Christ-Centered Healing for Wives of Combat* by Christopher B. Adsit, Rahnella Adsit, and Marshele Carter Waddell. This book offers comfort and practical help to the wives of combat veterans struggling with the hidden wounds of war, including PTSD. Insights from the medical and counseling community are wrapped in biblical principles and the shared experiences of other military wives.

For Children

- *Finding My Way: A Teen's Guide to Living with a Parent Who Has Experienced Trauma* by Michelle D. Sherman and DeAnne

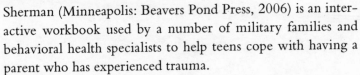

Sherman (Minneapolis: Beavers Pond Press, 2006) is an interactive workbook used by a number of military families and behavioral health specialists to help teens cope with having a parent who has experienced trauma.

- MilitaryOneSource, in conjunction with the Children's Television Network, developed several DVD resources to assist preschool children and adolescents cope with deployment-related stress. The *Sesame Street* video "Talk, Listen, Connect" covers deployments, homecomings, changes, and grief.
- The Army Pediatric community has been active in developing DVDs for elementary age children (*Mr. Po and Friends*) and teens (*Youth Coping with Military Deployment: Promoting Resilience in Your Family*). These materials are available for free download via the American Academy of Pediatrics website.

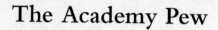

SEVENTEEN

The Academy Pew

Persevering through Loneliness

With man this is impossible, but with God all things are possible.

Matthew 19:26

Midway through my freshman year at the Air Force Academy, I hit rock bottom. My girlfriend from Brooklyn broke up with me, my grade point average was a dismal 1.4, and both my roommates quit. The pressure was too much for them. During a "training session," the upperclassmen yelled at us while we did push-ups and sang patriotic songs. My roommate Jimmy—a Texan, football player, and awesome guy—started trembling in the push-up position and then just got up and left.

Once a cadet quits, he or she is required to wear mixed pieces of uniform—green fatigues and black Corfam shoes. This Academy tradition makes you stand out as a quitter. Jimmy was my dear friend, and seeing him in that attire unnerved me. I was depressed when he gave up. The Air Force needed such men as Jimmy, and I was angry when they broke him. Why not encourage him to stay? Why not support him during his time of weakness? But that is not how it goes at the Air Force Academy. You must want to be there and work hard to graduate.

After Jimmy left, I called my parents to tell them that it was over: I wanted to come home. I felt isolated and alone. My mother told me in her broken English, "Hold on one minute, Raffaele. [My full name is Raffaele Antonio Monetti.] I want to read to you why you went to the Air Force Academy." She had the foresight to have me write down why I wanted to attend the Air Force Academy before I boarded my flight. She recited the words I had written on a cocktail napkin. (I still have that napkin.) My mother encouraged me to finish what I had started and to pray for strength. My mom, who did not want me to go into the military, was now encouraging me to persevere, even though it meant being away from family. Amazing! Her tone on the phone was resolute. I felt that my short Sicilian mother was now ten feet tall, grabbing me by the collar and kicking me in the rear.

That night, I went to the Cadet Chapel, sat in a deserted pew, and opened a Bible. I do not recall what I read, except that it was in a book of Peter. Next I got down on my knees and prayed for help. It was a simple prayer, but from the heart. While crying alone in the empty pews, I called upon God and then fell asleep, mentally and physically exhausted. Upon awaking hours later, I was startled to see it was so late, and I hurried back to Cadet Squadron 38. On my way across the desolate terrazzo under the starry Rocky Mountain night sky, I felt different. My mind was clear and an inner strength stirred within me. Hours earlier, I had entered the Cadet Chapel dejected and lonely. I exited the chapel as a thoroughbred ready to win the Kentucky Derby.

The upperclassmen were looking for me, for it was past curfew. As I entered the dorm room, they were on me like piranhas. "Monetti! Where have you been! Get your neck against the wall." I tried explaining, but they were not interested in hearing what I had to say. They expected me to play their game and recite the three standard responses, "Yes, Sir," "No, Sir," and "No Excuse, Sir," but not this time! Something had changed. I had changed. I was no longer afraid. I knew that I was not alone, and I knew that no matter what they said or did, I was going to make it. Just like that! I laughed at their feeble attempt to break me, and they knew I had crossed that bridge to success.

That day was one of the most important days in my life. Faith took on new meaning in my life. It became a faith in something bigger than myself. Faith requires believing in something you are unable to see but believe to be true nonetheless. My faith in God, and knowing that I was not alone, helped me overcome adversity. That faith would help me later during turbulent times in my life.

Military servicemen are made to endure extreme situations that require life-or-death decisions. The battlefield is filled with unique hazards and minefields, sometimes literally. In addition, the enemy looks for ways to discredit, demoralize, and defeat us. The enemy wants us to believe that we're all alone. We should not underestimate the enemy's resolve or capability. The threat is real and we must fight and defeat it. Giving up is not an option. We must persevere, continually showing up with our shields ready, our eyes vigilant for attacks, and our swords in hand to strike the enemy. If we lose faith in our resolve and second-guess why we fight, then the enemy wins.

When we voluntarily took our oath, we vowed to protect and defend the Constitution of the United States against all enemies, foreign and domestic. We must not lose sight of our duty. Perseverance will get us through this fight, just as it did our forefathers, who had to overcome incredible odds and defeat powerful enemy forces that threatened their way of life.

Perseverance is also required in other aspects of our lives. Thinking of quitting on your marriage? Don't give up. Thinking of quitting your job? Don't give up. Thinking of ending your life? Don't give up. Persevere—finish what you started. Take that next step. When I wanted to leave the Air Force Academy, I got down on my knees and asked for God's help to persevere, and God was there for me. He is there for you, too.

The upperclassmen who hounded and pushed me to the limit did so to see if I could deal with the pressure. When I realized that I could overcome their demands, due to my faith in God and self, I was able to laugh in their faces and succeed. Likewise, the enemy is in our faces, wanting us to quit. Faith provides the extra edge required to succeed: we are not alone.

The experience at the chapel helped define me as a person and brought me to understand the importance of perseverance and faith. I felt encouraged to go forward one more step, when everything else told me to stop. For the next four years while at the Air Force

Academy, I knew in my heart that with God all things were possible, and in His strength, I could do anything. I still believe that today. And if you have not experienced that strength, all you have to do is ask, and God will be there for you.

Lord, remind me daily to remember that you are by my side during the good and bad times, and that all things are possible with you. Help me to persevere when all seems lost.

HAVE YOU EVER HIT ROCK BOTTOM? Did you turn to God for His guidance and strength or away from Him? Are you lonely? What can you do right now to change your perspective and remind yourself that you are not alone?

EIGHTEEN

Get This Elephant Off My Head!

Lifting the Weight of Depression

*And if you faithfully obey the voice of the Lord your God
. . . all these blessings shall come upon you and overtake
you, if you obey the voice of the Lord your God.*
                    Deuteronomy 28:1–2 (ESV)

I viewed the opened day planner sitting on my nightstand that seemed to scream out the day's itinerary. I waged war with the thought of getting out of bed. The to-do list overwhelmed me— the appointments, the phone calls to make, the tasks to carry out for our restaurant and the organizations with which I was involved. Venturing from my bed's security would also force me to see the kitchen—but not the counter. I was sure my family's popcorn bowls and glasses from the previous evening would greet me, camouflaging the counter below.

Next, I would travel down the hall to discover mounting laundry demanding my attention. The clincher to anchor me under my warm covers was the hill of unattended mail. Oh, the bills, insurance forms to file, and banking statements to balance! Each weighty task inched me deeper into darkness. I felt like an invisible elephant rested on my head. I lost the physical strength to rise, knowing what awaited me beyond my bedroom door. I pulled the sheets over my head and surrendered to the sanctuary of my bed.

Several months earlier, I attacked each responsibility-loaded day with vigor, but presently Tony and I were struggling in our marriage. Our once sweet relationship became sour with discontent. Our oldest child was leaving for college out of state. Unattained dreams evolved into bitterness. Long missions, TDYs, and business responsibilities wedged Tony away from our family and the quality time to which we were accustomed. Our communication link severed. Tony faced retirement and was striving to control unknown circumstances. Whenever I mentioned touchy issues, Tony grew angry. I bottled my feelings to avoid conflict, compensating by overcommitting my time to several worthy organizations. I became distant and failed to meet Tony's needs, which caused him to feel unappreciated and unloved. In turn, Tony's dissatisfaction brewed and I grew more distant and depressed. We ignored the threatening conditions as we steadily rowed our relationship into the perfect storm.

Just because Christians commit their lives to Christ doesn't award them a "get out of problems free" card. It doesn't matter if you pastor a church, lead a Bible study, or write award-winning books on healthy marriages, the devil *knows* your personal weaknesses and methodically weaves his sticky web to cause chaos and destruction wherever he can. This is what happened to us. Although the "love" feelings seemingly disappeared, we both valued our marriage vows to each other and to God. If we were going live out the faith we professed, we needed to pocket our feelings and obey God's commands. We could not yield to the evil that was feasting on our marriage's discontent.

I called Christian friends and family members who I knew would earnestly pray for us. It's not easy sharing ugly personal truths, but we needed reinforcement to help save our collapsing marriage. Prayer support quickly became the buttress of our shaky marriage structure.

Tony and I lived at opposite ends of the house to avoid fighting. Our feelings of love for each other seemingly disappeared. I did the only thing left to do. I fell to my knees and pleaded with God to restore my feelings for my husband and rebuild our war-torn marriage. Exhausted from trying to solve our problems on our own, Tony finally agreed to marriage counseling.

A root canal was like a day at the spa compared to our counseling sessions, but our toxic relationship needed healing. Our marriage's last hope rested on going through the painful sessions. To avoid conflict, Tony and I would drive the one-hour trip in separate cars. I prayed for our counselors, Steve and Cheryl, that they could weather our stormy sessions. At one discouraging point, I asked Tony for a separation so our family could live peacefully while continuing counseling. Thankfully, Tony adamantly rejected my idea. Looking back, separating may have hammered the nails into a coffin for our marriage.

Through the thorny counseling sessions, Tony and I learned invaluable lessons about ourselves. Cheryl compared unmet relational needs to a sponge. When our desire for quality time, words of affirmation, understanding, touch, and time spent together are neglected, we become dried up, like a thirsty, hardened sea sponge. If someone strolls in and bull's-eyes that unmet need, it's as if that person holds a sprinkling can. Both Tony's and my sponge were rock hard. We needed to focus on watering each other's needs before someone else did. Years of communication neglect had left us wounded. We had to relearn how to talk to each other, and more importantly—*listen*.

Amazed that Steve didn't dart from his office to seek a new profession after our initial meetings, Tony and I gleaned priceless information that we use to this day. Steve asked that we pray daily to see ourselves as we *really* are. Often our minds possess cataracts when viewing our own flaws, but we magnify our spouse's imperfections with high-powered microscopes. We each began to focus on our own blemishes instead of each other's faults. I heard a guest on *Oprah* explain that individuals maintain three realities of who they are: how we perceive ourselves; how others see us; and who we really are. Counseling became a mirror to reveal the "real" us.

Mending our relationship required putting aside the fresh emotional wounds and standing on our marriage commitment to each other and to God. A friend coincidently gave me an inspirational book by Karen Kingsbury that uncannily portrayed my situation. (I've heard that coincidence is just God working anonymously. I am a believer!) When the book's main character recounted her married history, my icy heart melted. I reflected on my own marriage. Tony and I had shared three births and the death of our unborn child together. We experienced first steps, 2:00 a.m. fevers, Little

League, and piano recitals. We survived wars and life-threatening health scares, served community and country, wiped tears, and built a strong family. At one time, we were each other's best friend. We couldn't lose that. I set the tear-stained book on my nightstand and grabbed my laptop computer.

Tony was the keynote speaker at a weeklong aviation symposium in London. My mom, worried that I was teetering on the brink of a breakdown, had flown in to help me while Tony was away. Childcare was built in. I decided to prove my commitment to Tony through extreme action. I clicked on a travel site and booked a flight the following day to Great Britain. For the first time, I understood the *for worse* part of the marriage vows, and I promised God to love my husband even when the world's easy answer would be to bail out. I clicked on the airline's Submit button, and as my ticket processed, I submitted my marriage to God. Tough times awaited us, but I knew that with God's powerful guidance, we could find our way back to each other and the love we once shared.

Lord, help me to obey your commands when healthy emotions run dry and hope seems lost. Help me to see myself as I really am. Instill peace within me, and remind me that when I heed your commands, your blessings follow.

HAS YOUR MARRIAGE RELATIONSHIP FELT HOPELESS?
In what ways? What are your spouse's top relational needs? What actions are you implementing to safeguard your relationship from

future storms? Have you made a conscious choice to remain obedient to God's laws, even if love seems lost?

Resource

Operation Military Family helps military couples "battle ready" their relationships. They offer a couple's check-up, family assessments, and a battle-ready action plan. Learn more about this website in the Resource section at the back of this book.

NINETEEN

I Choose Us

When Love Disappears

What you decide on will be done, and light will shine on your ways.

                                                              Job 22:28

Fatigued from jet lag, I hurriedly scribbled a message on a white cocktail napkin and handed it to Andy, the young conference coordinator of London's annual aviation conference. Feeling like a junior high student, I asked Andy to secretly pass the note to Air Force Lieutenant Colonel Tony Monetti, who was presently captivating the audience with a B-2 bomber mission adventure. The audience's lengthy applause could be heard from the upstairs lobby.

Andy inconspicuously transferred the folded message to the colonel as the presentation ended. Tony read and reread the words written on the slightly torn napkin. His eyes searched the room. "Only my wife would write this. How did you get this note?" he asked

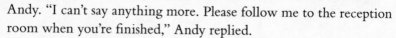

Andy. "I can't say anything more. Please follow me to the reception room when you're finished," Andy replied.

I love spontaneity; however, my actions bordered on crazy when I booked a flight from Missouri to London one day before departure in an effort to salvage my marriage. The exorbitant price (as much as my son's first college semester) due to the last-minute overseas booking, the ungodly 3:00 a.m. departure time, the eight-hour Houston layover, and the nine-hour flight seated next to a passenger who hacked and honked into tissues throughout the entire flight, was paradise compared to the last three months of marital misery that Tony and I inflicted upon each other.

As I anxiously waited for Tony to enter the reception room with the aeronautical executives who were already filtering in, verses from Isaiah 43 kept echoing in my thoughts: *Fear not . . . When you walk through the fire, you will not be burned . . . Do not be afraid, for I am with you* (vv. 1–2, 5). We sure had walked through some scorching flames lately, so burning hot that after nineteen years of marriage, our vocabulary sizzled with the word *divorce*. Each hurtful word fired forth like a burning bullet, searing the heart, leaving our once healthy union in peril. Hope camouflaged itself so well under the daily scornful conversations that reconciliation seemed impossible.

Tony followed Andy down the plush, red-carpeted stairs into the reception area where I waited, blocking my face from view with a London *Metro* newspaper. When I finally heard Tony's deep, soft voice, I slowly lowered the paper, revealing my presence. Tony took a deep breath, and several seconds passed before he exhaled. Processing his wife in London proved challenging, but when my identity finally registered, his face illuminated like a little boy's when lighting his first firework. He burst out, "Thank you, God," followed by, "You're completely nuts! I can't believe you are really here in London. My crazy wife!" He hurried past the silver-laden, white linen–covered tables, accidentally bumping into several distinguished men along his path, and embraced me tightly.

At that moment, all the past anguish and memories of terrible words spoken washed away. I knew the expensive plane ticket, the twenty-eight-hour sleep deficit, and every other annoyance and obstacle I encountered traveling to London was worth the priceless look on his face. At last, I had selected the right option. I *decided* to make our relationship work.

Decision-making ranks at the very bottom of my skills list. In fact, if only two entrees exist on a menu, I interrogate the waiter to ensure I make the best choice. No decision made before this moment had felt so right. Our deteriorating relationship demanded a show of serious commitment, assuring Tony that I wouldn't give up on our marriage. Traveling overseas to surprise him proved my serious commitment. Tony's smile widened as he triumphantly held up the wrinkled napkin like a first place trophy, displaying the words, *I CHOOSE US!* I borrowed that phrase from Tony's favorite movie, *The Family Man*. The main character, Jack Campbell, played by Nicholas Cage, is faced with choosing between two lives: a middle-class, blue-collar worker with a loving wife and children, or a lonely, high-powered business tycoon who lives in the lap of luxury. In the end, Jack says to his wife, "I choose us." Tony fully understood the volumes of unspoken meaning contained in those three small words.

During his half-hour break, Tony led me outside into the lush, colorful tulip garden, which accented the scenic Thames river flowing just beyond its borders. Riverboats waltzed upon the water's surface, transporting tourists to various destinations. The intermittent breeze renewed the light, fresh scent of hyacinth, just as the previous burst of fragrance from the bright pink and canary yellow flowers threatened to fade away. Then it happened. Tony looked deep into my eyes then passionately, yet softly, kissed me, burying layers of resentment and hurt. How did it happen? How did God pull this one off? How could my husband and I embrace in a loving kiss when just a few weeks ago, I never thought I could love again?

Only after *choosing* to honor our marriage commitment when the feelings of love disappeared did Christ revive our dying relationship. Many couples feel that their love for each other can never rekindle. Military life uniquely challenges marriage commitment due to TDYs, deployments, and the anxieties that accompanies moving every few years—all in addition to an already stress-bombarded society. But if God could take this hopeless couple and restore their lost love, He can do the same for you, but only if you choose to let Him.

Thank you, Lord, for caring about my relationships. Please help me remain obedient to you when times get tough and even seem hopeless. Help me to choose to love my spouse daily, even when I am worn out. Help me to express the importance and value he/she has in my life.

HAVE YOU EVER FELT like bailing out of your marriage commitment because it seemed hopeless? When was the last time you verbally expressed your pledge to love your spouse? Are you content with the status quo of your relationship? Have you asked God to restore loving feelings that may have become buried through time? Are you willing to choose to make your relationship work before the loving feelings return? What actions have you taken lately to strengthen your relationship?

Resource

Operation Military Family helps military couples "battle ready" their relationships. They offer a couple's check-up, family assessments, and a battle-ready action plan. Learn more about this website in the Resource section at the back of this book.

PART 4

Avoiding Destructive Behavior

TWENTY

Don't Play with Thunderstorms

Avoiding Risky Situations while Deployed

For the lips of an adulteress drip honey, and her speech is smoother than oil.

Proverbs 5:3

Pilots who play with thunderstorms run the risk of getting hit by lightning. Therefore, we do not play with thunderstorms! It is a simple rule most pilots understand, especially old graybeard pilots, those pilots who have been around a while. During my first cross-country solo flight in a T-38 supersonic Talon, while soaring over the glorious mountains of Utah, I observed a large thunderstorm in the distance. The weather briefer had warned me of the potential for thunderstorms along my flight route. He was right, as the large air mass in front of me churned like boiling water.

Rather than flying around it like I should have, I decided to fly above it. I asked Utah Center, an air traffic control center, for an unrestricted climb to forty-five thousand feet, the maximum altitude for the T-38, and they cleared me as requested. I started to climb, but the clouds raced up beneath me at the same rate of climb as the T-38. By God's grace, my jet beat the storms . . . but just barely. I know of a pilot who attempted the same foolishness in a T-38 and didn't live to tell his story. Playing with thunderstorms is irresponsible, unnecessary, and only leads to trouble. The same could be said of flirting with an adulteress.

Once during a trip, I met a beautiful blonde commercial pilot at the airport, and we struck up a conversation while waiting for our luggage. As we walked to the transportation area after retrieving our luggage, we discovered that we were staying at the same hotel. On the bus, we continued sharing flying stories and realized that we had a lot in common. I also could not help but notice Lisa's attractive physique. I shared that I was happily married and showed pictures of my family. Lisa instantly revealed that she was also married, but was having marital problems. I encouraged her to keep her family together and work things out. Once at the hotel, we parted ways.

Later I was surprised by a knock at my door. The pretty blonde, who had changed into clothing accentuating her shapely body even more, strolled into my room as if she belonged there. She seemed desperate and said that she just needed to talk with someone. When I asked how she knew my room number, she said that she noticed my room number while at the front desk.

Here was a beautiful woman in my room who likely had intentions other than just talking. Thoughts raced through my mind: "Perhaps she really wants to just talk. What's wrong with listening?"

"Have a great time, and no one would ever know." *"Get her outta here!"* I kept the door open and asked her to leave. Lisa said that I had it all wrong, she just wanted to talk. But I told her no and motioned with my hand for her to leave.

If I had shut the door with her inside my room, the short-term pleasure would not have outweighed the long-term consequences. I love my wife and betraying our marriage vows is a stain with which I could not live—not to mention that I would be sinning against God too, who told us, "You shall not commit adultery" (Exodus 20:14). On her way out, Lisa told me her room number, in case I changed my mind. She obviously had issues, but I am not a marriage counselor. I am a married man.

Many couples in good relationships think they are immune to marriage problems. Then temptation knocks, and they begin to entertain thoughts of infidelity. Steve Pringle, the executive director of Diakonos Counseling, says,

> Infidelity boils down to two powerful factors that influence both men and women to stray. First is lack of maturity, which shows itself in immediate gratification and strong self-centeredness with a lack of forward thinking. Second is an inability to overcome hurt feelings that result when emotional needs are not being met. The hurt spouse either intentionally or accidentally comes in contact with someone who begins to meet these needs, and the spouse allows "feel good" moods to control what he or she thinks or does. These "feel

good" moods often have the power to override the commonsense voice that warns us, "No, don't do that."[22]

Do you know if your spouse's needs are being met? Have you communicated your unmet needs to your spouse? Asking these questions can guard against infidelity.

Ask yourself another question. Of all the affairs that you're aware of, how many began as "just friends"? Many extramarital affairs seem to start off innocently with an acquaintance or a friend. To some married couples, having friends of the opposite sex is no big deal. I beg to differ. My personal rule is simple. I do not have female friends that I "hang out" with (nor does Penny have male friends that she goes out with for coffee or shopping). This is one way to affair-proof a marriage.

When deployed for long periods of time, the potential for extramarital affairs increases. Soldiers who mix the effects of loneliness and the attitude of "what goes TDY, stays TDY" especially need to watch out. The thunderstorm is always active and brewing and just waiting for the right conditions to explode. Servicemen who behave one way at home and another way when deployed lose respect of their fellow teammates. Their integrity is tarnished because it is difficult to respect a person who cannot honor his or her marital commitment.

If you and your spouse are not meeting each other's needs, then maybe it is best to seek professional guidance. A seasoned marriage counselor can mend broken relationships. By meeting your spouse's emotional and physical needs, your marriage will grow stronger, but

---

22. Steve Pringle's comment, given in an interview on May 31, 2010, is used by permission.

the process requires time and commitment. My dear departed friend, Virgil Dearduff, who was married for nearly sixty years, used to say of a successful marriage, "You have to keep working at it every day." I still smile at his wisdom. Marriage takes work, but it is well worth persevering through difficult times and overcoming adversities.

Instead of going elsewhere to have your needs met, work at the relationship to which you are committed. Spice up your marriage in creative ways. Start with some basics like getting in shape so you look good for yourself and your spouse. How about grooming and smelling good before intimate time? How about figuring out what you can do for your spouse? (Hint: It does not involve buying cheap lingerie.) The challenge is to find creative ways to make the relationship work.

Going elsewhere to seek personal satisfaction is not the answer. Affairs are selfish and destructive to your relationships with family, friends, and God. If you have already flown into that storm, then fly straight and level and get out as quickly as possible. Although the speech of an adulteress "is smoother than oil" (Proverbs 5:3), it will ultimately leave a sour taste in your mouth that lasts forever. Do the right thing and get out of the situation now.

Having an affair is like playing with thunderstorms. If you do, you might get struck by lightning. So do not play with thunderstorms! Just do not go there.

Lord, give me the strength to make wise choices. Help me avoid the temptation of having an extramarital affair. Give me the fortitude to do the right thing.

DO YOU PLAY WITH THUNDERSTORMS? Are you the type of person who has flirtatious talks with people of the opposite sex? When you are away from home, do you act differently? Are you contemplating having an affair? How can you protect your marriage from thunderstorms?

TWENTY-ONE

Your Father-in-Law Called

Safeguarding Your Relationship

He must also have a good reputation with outsiders, so that he will not fall into disgrace and into the devil's trap.

1 Timothy 3:7

"Someone just called, I think he said he was your father-in-law, but I'm not sure because of his foreign accent," Brent said as he searched for his car keys. "Oh my gosh, that *was* my father-in-law. Great! How will I explain a man's voice answering the phone at 10:30 p.m.?" My mind scrambled. "I'm dead! No matter what I say, he's going to think the worst. His son is overseas risking his life and now he thinks his daughter-in-law is unfaithful. I'm not sure I can fix this one," I told Brent.

Brent had graciously offered to stay at my house to watch my son, Nico, while I drove the babysitter home after our Friday night Bible study. This way I wouldn't have to awaken my two-year-old and then spend the next hour trying to coax him back to sleep. It was innocent enough, but for my father-in-law, the situation must have appeared questionable. My father-in-law did not understand the attraction of Bible study and certainly did not approve of a man being in his daughter-in-law's home while his son defended our country overseas. The painted picture did not look good. The only thing I could do was to call him back and try my best to explain the situation.

Part of me resented having to defend myself for something I did not do, but my overprotective Italian father-in-law was old school. The way the situation appeared, it would be difficult for anyone not to perceive the worst. Even though I held low hopes of my father-in-law understanding the situation, I had to try. I dialed the number, and my father-in-law picked up the receiver before the first ring finished. I attempted to dig myself out of an untrue scenario. He sincerely thanked me for returning his call after he heard my story.

To this day I still don't know if he believes me, but I placed myself in my husband's combat boots. If I were called away from my family for an extended time and phoned my home at 10:30 at night and a woman's voice answered, regardless of how innocent it was, my mind would instantly doubt my husband's faithfulness. Doubt is an ugly precursor to jealousy and mistrust. Both can destroy a marriage, and divorce is increasingly becoming the home front's newest casualty of war.

Looking back, having a man alone in my home was not a good idea. Not only for the misconception it evoked, but because *all* men have sexual drives. This is something I've come to realize as I've "matured" in age (and hopefully in wisdom also). Naively placing myself in a situation where I am alone with a man may cause him to be tempted, even though my intentions are innocent. I know many women who become lonely after months of no male companionship. When they find themselves alone with a man who is not their husband, temptation knocks at their door as well.

I realize some readers may be saying, "Hey, my spouse trusts me. I can be alone with the opposite sex without a problem." The motto that my husband and I stand by is "avoid the situation." Friendships with the opposite sex are not healthy for your marriage. Having coffee with a male friend, although innocent, may open the door for a relationship to start later on. You may think it harmless at the time, but he is having other thoughts, and they are not about swapping recipes!

My son Nico, who is in college, called me last night. He was surprised that a potential girlfriend would not allow him to sleep at her apartment, even though he had no intentions of making sexual advancements. Her refusal to allow him to stay the night forced Nico to drive several hours. First he would drive an hour and a half to her college after working late to see her, and then he would drive the lengthy return trip back home when he may be tired. Staying overnight to avoid driving while tired made complete sense to him; however, this girl refused to blemish her reputation by creating a false perception. I expressed that this girl was worth pursuing and proceeded to tell him about Brent and the babysitting situation that caused so much havoc.

Job-related demands throw stress on our deployed men and women, and meeting those demands requires one-mindedness and concentration. Doubt is a grenade that wounds healthy marriages and distracts warriors from the tasks that accompany defending our country and staying safe. Assuring your spouse with words and, more importantly, actions that your marriage is free from infidelity keeps war from spreading to the home front.

Lord, please help my actions reflect my faithfulness to my spouse. Help me to overcome imagining untrue situations due to loneliness. Plant friends in my life to keep me accountable when loneliness does prevail. If temptation confronts me, give me the wisdom to quickly walk away and lean on you for strength.

DO YOUR ACTIONS reassure your spouse that he or she is the first person you wake up thinking about and your last thought before going to bed each night? Looking back, have you ever planted seeds of doubt or mistrust by naive actions? What changes can you make in your relationship to strengthen each other's trust? How do you reassure your spouse that your marriage is secure?

Let's Go Yankees

Combating Pornography

No temptation has seized you except what is common to man. And God is faithful; he will not let you be tempted beyond what you can bear. But when you are tempted, he will also provide a way out so that you can stand up under it.

1 Corinthians 10:13

"Let's go Yanks! Let's go Yanks!" the crowd roared, as the New York Yankees battled in the playoffs. Above the noise of the crowd, a friend invited me to a gentlemen's club after the game. "The ladies there are beautiful and completely naked!" He smirked and slyly winked. Part of me wanted to go and have a good time with the boys.

Perhaps you have been in similar situations, particularly when deployed. When deployed, servicemen continue to have certain needs and viewing pornography helps meet that need. Pornography is a common struggle for servicemen, regardless of religious beliefs or backgrounds, though most Christians feel uncomfortable talking about it. I understand, because I faced challenges with pornography, and wish to share some thoughts, as this obstacle distracted me from reaching peace with God and myself for some time.

During a Christian rally put on by Promise Keepers, an organization dedicated to uniting men to become passionate followers of Jesus Christ, the speaker addressing the thousands in attendance told a startling story. He asked the hotel receptionist if the amount of pornography viewed in the hotel—booked primarily by Promise Keeper men—was less, the same, or more than usual. The response stunned the audience. The amount was more than usual. I was relieved to know that other Christian men dealt with this issue.

Often an internal strife emerges between my desire to follow Christ and my ability to control lust. I know what the right thing to do is; however, it is my basic instinct to look. So, what's a man to do? First, I had to admit that this behavior is wrong. Jesus said, "You have heard that it was said, 'Do not commit adultery.' But I tell you that anyone who looks at a woman lustfully has already committed adultery with her in his heart" (Matthew 5:27–28). After accepting that truth, I then developed and committed to a plan of action. What works for me is a strategy of developing strong habits to avoid the situation and knowing the truth behind the exploitative business of pornography.

As pilots, we use the technique of "chair flying" to visualize a successful mission. When chair flying, pilots envision crunch points that are likely to occur during flight. Crunch points are times in flight when many things happen at once, requiring pilots to preplan actions. For example, a takeoff is a crunch point because pilots have to transition from the runway control tower airspace to air traffic control airspace while flying and changing configuration (e.g., getting landing gear and flaps up). By doing so, pilots preprogram their decision-making process to better confront emergencies and unforeseen circumstances when actually airborne. Similarly, when temptation knocks, and it will, I predetermine to remove myself from the environment. I walk away. By avoiding the situation, temptations are deflected.

Today, it is too easy to access pornography to meet your particular fantasy. Some of my friends curb their ability to view Internet pornography through family-friendly software or by blocking certain cable channels. Others place computers in centralized family locations. The key is to develop solutions for avoiding the probability of viewing pornography before it occurs.

Another technique that works is letting my wife know of my temptation. By being honest with Penny that I have certain needs, she is able to understand me. Likewise, I try to meet her needs, too, by taking her out for dinner or shopping, or offering a foot massage. The point is, let your spouse know of your challenges, for your spouse can help. I am grateful that Penny understands and helps meet my needs; however, I am mindful that my wife is not an object just there to satisfy my needs. She is my wife and I love and respect her.

The ladies "used" in the pornography business are not respected. The ugly truth is that the women dancing naked or performing sex scenes on the Internet are doing so out of desperation. They resort to demeaning work to meet short-term, monetary needs. Some are forced into the industry. It is sad to think that girls my daughter's age are doing such acts. These ladies are daughters, mothers, and sisters.

Christian servicemen cannot in good conscience support this industry that degrades women. I used to justify that viewing porn was no big deal, but that was just a lie. When I look at myself in the mirror and walk away, I want my words to match my actions. As James 1:23–25 says, "Anyone who listens to the word but does not do what it says is like a man who looks at his face in a mirror and, after looking at himself, goes away and immediately forgets what he looks like. But the man who looks intently into the perfect law that gives freedom, and continues to do this, not forgetting what he has heard, but doing it—he will be blessed in what he does." Doing the right thing requires discipline and commitment, but the reward is peace with God and self.

The discipline of body and spirit is crucial when overcoming the sin of pornography. Developing healthy patterns helps me overcome temptation. Working out at the gym and engaging in sports helps relieve stress and has a side benefit of getting my body in shape. I work out six days a week. It takes self-control to find an hour daily, but I make time for myself.

I supplement my physical workouts with spiritual exercises. Staying in the Scriptures daily, attending church weekly, and getting involved with Bible studies are all positive activities that strengthen my spiritual walk with the Lord. Each morning, I read a chapter from the book of Proverbs based on the day's date (e.g., on May 5, I read Proverbs chapter 5) and one chapter from the Gospels (i.e., Matthew, Mark, Luke, and John). Key Scriptures, once memorized, can help deflect temptation (see Scripture Resources at the end of this chapter). Meeting with other Christian men and accountability partners that share common challenges can assist in overcoming this obstacle as well.

Pornography is a problem for many servicemen. If pornography challenges you, take heart, for we are not alone! However, accessing pornography for some becomes a form of addiction, which in turn adversely affects the individual and family. Professional counselors, chaplains, and institutions can help you and your family.

After admitting that viewing pornography is a sin, I developed a strategy that works for me. The key is having self-control and remaining committed to my convictions. Doing the right thing is not easy. But I do know that it brings me the greatest pleasure when I am at peace with God and doing the right thing. The short-term pleasure of looking at pornography is like a slow decay of my bones, whereas walking straight with the Lord lifts my spirit. As the Scriptures say, God provides an opportunity to escape temptation (see 1 Corinthians 10:13). Do not give up. You are not alone. Stay strong!

Lord God, thank you for providing a way out and giving me the strength to walk away when temptation arises. Help me to share my struggles with those who can help keep me accountable.

DO YOU STRUGGLE WITH PORNOGRAPHY? What avoidance techniques work for you? Have you discussed these issues of temptation with your spouse or Christian counselors?

Resource

Every Man's Battle is a website through New Life Ministries (NLM) that offers online support groups, workshops, and other resources to help win the war on sexual temptation one battle at a time. In response to the loneliness of the soldier who is away from home, NLM created the Every Soldier's Battle campaign, which provides military personnel, both home and abroad, with resources that will help soldiers who choose to maintain sexual integrity and sexual purity. NLM's goal is to provide ten thousand soldiers with an Every Soldier's Battle kit.

Scripture Resources

- How can a young man keep his way pure? By living according to your word. I seek you with all my heart; do not let me stray from your commands. I have hidden your word in my heart that I might not sin against you. (Psalm 119:9–11)
- She will give birth to a son, and you are to give him the name Jesus, because he will save his people from their sins. (Matthew 1:21)
- No temptation has seized you except what is common to man. And God is faithful; he will not let you be tempted beyond what you can bear. But when you are tempted, he will also provide a way out so that you can stand up under it. (1 Corinthians 10:13)
- I can do everything through him who gives me strength. (Philippians 4:13)

- For this reason he had to be made like his brothers in every way, in order that he might become a merciful and faithful high priest in service to God, and that he might make atonement for the sins of the people. Because he himself suffered when he was tempted, he is able to help those who are being tempted. (Hebrews 2:17–18)

- Therefore, since we have a great high priest who has gone through the heavens, Jesus the Son of God, let us hold firmly to the faith we profess. For we do not have a high priest who is unable to sympathize with our weaknesses, but we have one who has been tempted in every way, just as we are—yet was without sin. Let us then approach the throne of grace with confidence, so that we may receive mercy and find grace to help us in our time of need. (Hebrews 4:14–16)

- Blessed is the man who perseveres under trial, because when he has stood the test, he will receive the crown of life that God has promised to those who love him. When tempted, no one should say, "God is tempting me." For God cannot be tempted by evil, nor does he tempt anyone; but each one is tempted when, by his own evil desire, he is dragged away and enticed. Then, after desire has conceived, it gives birth to sin; and sin, when it is full-grown, gives birth to death. Don't be deceived, my dear brothers. (James 1:12–16)

- Submit yourselves, then, to God. Resist the devil, and he will flee from you. Come near to God and he will come near to you. Wash your hands, you sinners, and purify your hearts, you double-minded. (James 4:7–8)

- I write to you, fathers, because you have known him who is from the beginning. I write to you, young men, because you are strong, and the word of God lives in you, and you have overcome the evil one. (1 John 2:14)

TWENTY-THREE

Dog Puke and Celebrities

Dismantling Emotional Land Mines

Search me, O God, and know my heart; test me and know my anxious thoughts. See if there is any offensive way in me, and lead me in the way everlasting.

Psalm 139:23–24

I searched for the barely audible ringing phone, muffled further by kids bickering. "It's my turn to play. You died! Mommm, Nico won't give me a turn," whined my eight-year old son, Antonio. "Mom, listen to my side," retorted my twelve-year-old lawyer. "It took three weeks to get to this level. If I stop now, I have to start all over." *Brrrrring*, the squelched ringing sound squeezed through the argument's short-lived lull. "Does *anyone* know where the phone is?" I asked. "Here it is, Mommy." My four-year-old, peanut butter–faced daughter proudly held up a brownish goo and jelly-covered receiver. "I'm making us dinner," she proclaimed. *Brrrrring*. I rushed to the sticky phone as I spied my chocolate Lab's body arching up and down, sandwiched between the couch and the wall. "Someone get Rocky, quick! Take him outside. He's going to throw up!" Nico replied, "Make Antonio do it. I just have one more level . . ."

"Hello?" I hoped my voice's urgency would cue the caller to send a rescue squad. "Cough, hack, cough," echoed from the corner. In unison, all three kids screamed, "Ewww. Rocky! Gross! Pewww!" and then, moments away from reaching the prized level, the Benedict Arnolds joined forces and dashed upstairs. "Get back here, guys!" My command landed only on my sick dog's perked-up ears. "Hello? Anyone there?" A voice squeaked from the forgotten phone. "Oh, sorry," I apologized as I examined my gooey, peanut butter–covered hands. Struggling to balance the phone between my neck and ear, I dragged our stubborn dog into the frigid cold air. The New York accent bellowed, "You're going to have to talk louder. There's loud music blaring in the background."

Tony was chosen to support an NFL Super Bowl B-2 flyby.[23] He called from sunny Florida to check in as he routinely did when he flew TDY stateside. "We were invited to the pregame gala party," he said. "Can you hear Ricky Martin singing live? Listen." Tony must have nearly been on stage because a deafening "She Bangs" boomed into the receiver. He continued, "I just met the cast from *Everybody Loves Raymond*. The woman who plays the mother-in-law is really cool. Her grandson loves the B-2. The buffet is out of this world: caviar, shrimp, crab, and prime rib. Phenomenal! How are things at home?"

---

23. A flyby is a low altitude flight over a specific location, usually in front of spectators.

Long silence. I debated whether to hang up and blame it on a bad connection, but no, that would be lying. Maybe I should rant on about the last twenty minutes of home-front war so Tony could feel a smidgen of guilt for having fun while I manned the domestic battlefield. No, that would be cruel. I didn't want to ruin his good time. I chose my words carefully: "Honey, I'm glad the military occasionally gives you awesome perks like Super Bowl parties, meeting TV stars and professional athletes, exquisite food, travel, and air shows. You definitely deserve the fringe benefits for your selfless sacrifices, but honestly, I struggle to share your excitement while wiping up our sick dog's puke. Could you call me back in one hour? I promise to ooze with excitement then. Deal?" Tony, knowing me for over thirteen years then, realized it would be best to call me later.

During military life, home-front spouses experience separations of many varieties, causing a roller coaster of emotions. You feel pride that your loved one is serving but may resent that you are left at home with all the responsibilities. Then you feel guilty for feeling resentful. Emotions left unattended can take a marriage through dangerous twists. After I cleaned the dog vomit, a stain remained. I contacted the carpet cleaner for quick removal. After my husband called to share his excitement with me, a bitter residue stuck to my spirit. I shamefully resented that I was stuck cleaning dog puke while my husband chummed around with celebrities. I knew that resentment injures relationships, so I hauled my dirt to the ultimate cleaner of emotional filth—the Lord. I set my loathsome emotions at His feet, and then shared my feelings with Tony when he returned home. Tony listened, and surprisingly understood my feelings. Consequently, he became more sensitive and encouraged me to break away to meet with friends and take annual rejuvenating TDYs myself.

If negative emotions resulting from military life stressors such as loneliness, relocation, sacrificed careers, war and deployment anxieties, and single-parenting frustrations (to name just a few) are not addressed at their onset, sizzling fuses may ignite a relationship explosion later. Shards in the form of depression, anger, alcohol and/ or drug abuse, extramarital affairs, physical illness, and other emotional fallout are remnants of neglected communication.

Tony and I look back and laugh fondly at the Super Bowl/dog puke incident. The episode is a reminder of how to communicate honestly about the seemingly little things.

Heavenly Father, thank you for your unconditional love. Please make me aware of unresolved emotions that prevent me from being the kind of partner, parent, and friend that you want me to be. Help me to express my feelings effectively, and heal my heart from past hurts.

WHAT EMOTIONS DO YOU BATTLE and seek to conquer? What actions have you taken to address them? How can you avoid emotional explosions in the future?

TWENTY-FOUR

Wake-up Call

The Realities of Alcohol Abuse

Do not get drunk on wine, which leads to debauchery. Instead, be filled with the Spirit.

Ephesians 5:18

One year I threw a surprise birthday party for Penny. The party was a blast. Each friend brought a specialty drink or food; however, someone made an alcoholic drink that went down smooth but had disastrous aftereffects. Before I knew it, I had had too much to drink.

The next morning was awful. Penny was unhappy that I drank too much, and I was not in the mood to hear her complaints while nursing a hangover. We had an appointment that morning, and I asked her to drive. As she steered the car along the winding roads, I started to feel sick. We made our way back home, and I went straight to bed—went to the toilet a few times too, I may add.

Drinking alcohol in excess is stupid. I hurt myself, my wife, and my kids, who were home during the party. That night was a wake-up call. I stopped drinking hard alcohol. Years later, I stopped drinking altogether. I stopped because I grew up. I was honest with myself and realized that every time I did or said something I regretted later, alcohol was *always* involved.

Drinking alcohol is part of the military's heritage. How many movies portray soldiers slamming down whiskey shots after completing a life-threatening mission? But just like other destructive behaviors, drinking can get out of hand and become an addiction. A close friend of mine is a recovering alcoholic. Alcoholics have a strong craving for alcohol and an inability to control their alcohol intake. For them, there is no such thing as just one drink. My friend shared how he would wake up after a night of drinking and not know what had occurred the previous day. He reached a point where he nearly lost his family and job, but he *finally* admitted his alcohol problem and entered rehabilitation.

I have witnessed many returning war zone veterans rely on alcohol to numb the pain of their experiences. In addition to abusing alcohol, warriors resort to other means of masking stress, such as prescription and illegal drugs. Although the majority of soldiers do not use illegal drugs, many drink alcohol. It is acceptable, legal, and even encouraged.

Families and careers are damaged and some destroyed by alcohol, but there is help. Each military unit has a welfare center staffed with knowledgeable professionals. Other resources include the military medical clinic, the Department of Veterans Affairs, chaplains, and your unit's supervisors.

In my case, alcohol has a negative effect on my behavior and can lead to regret. The rewards do not outweigh the benefits. As a Christian, I value my walk with God and do not want to be labeled a hypocrite. It is tough for people to take you seriously when you share God's message reeking of beer or bourbon.

Today I have a great time socializing knowing that my mind is clear, my conscience is clean, and my spirit is filled with joy because I am doing the right thing and still enjoying life fully.

Lord, help me be consistent in my walk with you. Fill me with your Holy Spirit and give me the courage to do the right thing all the time.

DO YOU DRINK EXCESSIVELY? If so, have you admitted your need for help to the Lord? Have you confided in your spouse, a chaplain, or a Christian counselor?

Resource

Learn more about Alcoholics Anonymous in the Resources section in the back of this book.

Scripture Resources

- Do not get drunk on wine, which leads to debauchery. Instead, be filled with the Spirit. (Ephesians 5:18)
- Wine is a mocker and beer a brawler; whoever is led astray by them is not wise. (Proverbs 20:1)
- Let us behave decently, as in the daytime, not in orgies and drunkenness, not in sexual immorality and debauchery, not in dissension and jealousy. (Romans 13:13)
- Deacons, likewise, are to be men worthy of respect, sincere, not indulging in much wine, and not pursuing dishonest gain. (1 Timothy 3:8)

TWENTY-FIVE

I'll Just Buy This One Thing

Combating Destructive Behaviors

Therefore, prepare your minds for action; be self-controlled; set your hope fully on the grace to be given you when Jesus Christ is revealed.

1 Peter 1:13

Her name was Meg. Big car. Big wallet. *Big* sweet tooth for shopping. I didn't know her personally, but her reputation for out-of-control spending preceded her. Whenever Meg's husband deployed, her spending habits were as controlled as a starving Italian released into in a room full of pasta. I heard comments such as, "If you write Meg, make sure to include 'In Care of Macy's' in the address," and "Meg's credit card debt could compete with the national deficit!" Although spoken in jest, the comments weren't far off target (except for the federal deficit remark). Her shopping compulsion strangled her finances, and marriage disaster loomed like a circling vulture.

Thinking Meg's story to be an isolated case, I was sadly proven wrong. I found that not only do many spouses run up excessive debt when their honeys deploy, many also indulge in a myriad of destructive behaviors such as emotional eating, anorexia, drinking excessively, abusing prescription drugs, gambling, and infidelity (to name a few). What's a spouse to do?

Self-control is the sword that slays beastly behaviors. But first, the stalking enemy must be smoked out of its foxhole and identified. Refusing to admit that an enemy exists means it cannot be eliminated. Heavy-duty denial is a common denominator in every type of addiction.

How do you identify a destructive behavior? Ask yourself the following questions that were derived from the American Psychiatric Association's diagnostic criteria.[24]

- Do I immediately engage in this behavior to pull me out of a gloomy mood or relieve feelings of helplessness, guilt, anxiety, or depression?
- Do I get restless or irritable when I try to slow down or stop the behavior?
- Do I hide this behavior from loved ones and friends and lie about it when asked?
- Do I experience shame after engaging in the behavior?
- Do I spend increasing amounts of money or increase participation in the activity to receive the desired amount of pleasure?

---

24. American Psychiatric Association, *Diagnostic and Statistical Manual of Mental Disorders*, 4th ed. (Washington, DC: The Association, 1994).

- Do I spend time reliving past experiences or thinking about this behavior when I am not engaging in it?
- After I lose money, do I return to "get even" or recoup the lost funds?
- Have I ever stolen money or committed fraud or forgery to fund the behavior?
- Have I ever jeopardized or lost a significant relationship, job, or educational/career opportunity because of the activity?
- Have I ever relied on others to provide money to relieve a desperate financial situation caused by the activity?
- Have I repeatedly tried to stop or cut back on the behavior with no success?

Answering yes to five or more of these questions indicates pathological involvement with the activity. Three or four positive answers indicate a problem with the activity. If you answered yes to one or two questions, the behavior is at risk for becoming addictive.

Once the problem is out in the open, only then can a plan of action be created and executed to overcome it. If you struggle with a destructive behavior and have recognized a problem, the fact that you have continued reading this chapter is a very good sign. Even if you don't struggle with a destructive behavior, the following proactive steps will help all spouses maintain healthy well-being and avoid destructive behaviors.

Just as your body requires vitamins to function effectively, the mind requires a steady diet of affirmations to remain optimistic. If Christ loved us enough to surrender His life for us, shouldn't we honor His sacrifice by loving who He created and stop wounding ourselves with negative thought patterns? Proverbs 23:7 states, "For as he thinks in his heart, so is he" (NKJV). Our thoughts steer our actions. Bathe your mind in optimistic thoughts: read inspirational material and stories about heroes triumphing over life's obstacles. Compliment yourself out loud on an accomplishment, giving thanks to the One who made it possible. We certainly have no trouble dragging our minds into the mental boxing ring and throwing punches at our confidence when we mess up. Try something different. Pat yourself on the back when you get it right! Get rid of negative influences. Limit watching the news. Stay away from it altogether when you are in an anxious mood. Stories of heinous acts and devastation weigh the spirit down. Stay connected with encouraging friends. Every outfit has at least one "negative Nellie" in the group. If a friend's dismal outlook discourages you, and your cheery attitude won't change her petrified pout, continue to include Nellie in events, but expand your social circle to include cheerful, encouraging friends.

If you struggle with temptation, recruit an accountability partner who will help keep you on track. Join an online military spouses' network. Numerous website forums encompass all service branches and aspects of military life (see Resources at the end of this chapter). Forum topics span from emotional eating to the right amount to tip a commissary bagger. In these online gatherings, military spouses share fears, gather information, and receive needed encouragement—confidentially.

Staying physically healthy and active is another key to well-being. I know, you're thinking, *Not this worn-out topic again.* Stay with me. One of the best ways to combat stress is with a healthy diet, rest, and exercise. Many spouses whose honeys are deployed graze or gorge when stressed. Then two weeks before their spouses return, they dive into dangerous fad diets to shed the unwanted pounds. When their honeys step off the aircraft tanned, muscular, and twenty pounds trimmer than when they deployed, many spouses experience self-loathing, insecurity, or depression. Commit to trash the junk food now. Carve out eight hours for sleep. Switch to decaffeinated beverages. Take it from a prior caffeine junkie who took insomnia medication for four years: after I survived the short-lived withdrawal headaches, switched to a healthy diet (no fast food), and prioritized daily exercise in my crammed schedule, I chucked my meds and kissed 3:00 a.m. wake-ups good night.

Exercise however it fits into your planner. Find time! Women are famous for taking care of everyone else's needs and neglecting their own. Military fitness centers offer nutritional guidance, personal trainers (that cost major buckolas in the civilian world), and oodles of classes, from self-defense to the Latin cardio craze, Zumba. If babysitting issues challenge you, many fitness centers offer free or discounted child care for spouses of deployed soldiers. Visit base childcare facilities or start a babysitting co-op group to swap exercise time with fellow spouses. Include your children in your workout. Buy a running stroller. Indulge in family activities like bike riding, hiking, and swimming. Military.com offers a web page entitled "Spouse and Family Fitness." You'll be astounded at the array of spouse support on this site.

Spiritual balance completes the healthy spouse's profile. An active prayer life keeps the "what ifs" out of the backyard and brings peace into hectic lives. If you've never prayed before, not to worry. Talk to God as you would talk to your best friend. Soon enough, He will be. Share your doubts and vent your anxieties. Memorize Scripture relevant to you. Tape the verses to your mirror, refrigerator, and car dashboard for daily inspiration. Biblegateway.com is an excellent resource for finding Bible verses based on key words. *Our Daily Bread* (odb.org) offers encouragement through daily online devotionals. Attend a small group Bible study at the military chapel or local church. Don't quit searching if a church doesn't interest you—keep checking out churches until you find the right one for you and your family.

As 1 Peter 1:13 states, self-control requires *action*. Self-control is not a luxurious limousine in which one sits back to enjoy the ride; self-control is more like a NASCAR race machine that requires focused attention and constant maintenance to reach top performance. Conquering destructive behaviors to achieve a healthy mind, body, and spirit requires action—specifically, commitment. Commit yourself to action. If your destructive behavior evolves into an alcohol or drug addiction, part of your action plan may involve seeking professional counsel. Only you know.

I recently heard that Meg downsized to a mini coupe. She admitted that spending money was hurting herself and those she loved most. She enrolled in Dave Ramsey's class to achieve financial freedom and joined a local church's care group for addictive behaviors. Others no longer tease Meg—now her military sisters see her as a rock of strength that gives them hope.

Heavenly Father, reveal the areas in my life where I lack self-control. Lead me to encouraging friends, and help me to realize that the inner strength to conquer my weaknesses comes from you.

DO YOU CURRENTLY STRUGGLE FOR CONTROL? In what areas? What strategy will help you overcome your weaknesses? Do you know anyone struggling with destructive behaviors? What steps can you take to help lead them to recovery?

Resources

Military.com's web page entitled "Spouse and Family Fitness" is available at http://www.military.com/fitness-center/military -fitness/spouse-family/archive. Christian Military Wives, Military SOS (Significant Other Support), and Milspouse.com are support and information resources for military spouses of all Armed Force branches. Learn more about these organizations and websites in the Resources section in the back of this book.

PART 5

Communication

TWENTY-SIX

C = D

Seeing Ourselves as We Really Are

A happy heart makes the face cheerful, but heartache crushes the spirit.

Proverbs 15:13

My daughter slept in this morning and when she awoke, she was livid. Gabriella is a strong-willed child and maintains a straight-A average. Her being late to school resulted in earthquake-like conditions at home. I made it my goal to get her to smile during our ride to school. I attempted various methods to catch a smile, everything from singing Billy Joel songs out of tune to making funny faces, but nothing seemed to work. She just sat in her seat with a scrunched up face, puckered lips, and crossed arms. Then I remembered that just the other day, Gabriella ran up the stairs acting foolishly while unaware of the presence of a visiting friend. When I reminded her of that story, she turned her head and cracked a smile. Sometimes there is nothing funnier than laughing at yourself. The episode reminded me that not long ago, I acted childish too.

Years ago, Penny and I experienced a tumultuous time in our marriage, as a perfect storm brewed at the Monetti household. We were on opposite sides of the spectrum. I focused on preparing our family for my career change from the Air Force. Penny struggled with figuring out what she wanted from life, now that our children were older. My focus remained on providing for our family, and I expected Penny to get a full-time job and spend less time on what I considered trivial. Penny grew distant and our love life suffered. I was angry at her callousness toward me and kept reaching out for her. The more I tried, the worse things seemed to get.

The thought that my marriage was on the rocks deeply unsettled me. Penny suggested we see a marriage counselor to assist our stressed relationship. I vowed, in a rather theatrical way, that meeting with a marriage counselor was completely out of the question. I recall standing at the foot of the bed while pointing a finger and declaring, "Read my lips, C = D, and that means counseling equals divorce." I repeated *C equals D*, much like a child throwing a tantrum at a checkout register. The line in the sand was drawn. But God had other plans.

Without getting into the details, reality hit home one day, and I accepted that we needed third-party assistance. That is when Penny and I met a great man, Steve Pringle of Diakonos Counseling. He has a gift of gently providing solutions to complex problems. Steve somehow weaved love back into our lives. He listened to our differing points of view and provided outstanding Christian counseling, resulting in a saved marriage.

My first meeting with Steve was quite memorable. When I stepped out of his office, three ladies in the waiting room appeared nervous to sit by me, for I had just "opened up, Italian style" on Steve. After entering the counseling room, I unloaded my pent-up emotions. I was angry for our current predicament and let Steve know about it. I think everyone in the building heard it too.

Over the next year, and after coming to grips with certain truths, we resolved our differences and our marriage has blossomed. The counseling sessions with Steve helped me *see myself as I truly am* and not who I thought myself to be. I was controlling in our marriage, which isolated Penny. I was angry about trivial matters and had too high expectations on what Penny should be doing with her life. I was wrong for trying to control her and had to loosen my grip.

A good friend once shared that your spouse is like a bird. You cannot put your hands over a bird's wings and expect it to fly. You have to let go, and if the bird loves you, it returns. Through counseling, Penny came to grips with her own issues. We went through a healing process that involved forgiveness and reconciliation. Together, with the help of Steve and the Lord, we are once again dancing the dance of life together.

Today, it is easy to pinpoint where we went wrong in our marriage, but when you are in the thick of conflict, it is difficult to see things as they really are. A seasoned marriage counselor can help mend broken relationships, as long as you are both willing to show up and be open to change. Steve taught us the importance of effective communication and of understanding each other's point of view. Often when couples experience serious marriage problems, the individuals involved are too consumed with their own point of view. It's as if both parties are pulling in opposite directions on the same rope. When those people stop pulling, stress is reduced and they can meet in the middle.

As a military person, if you are anything like me, you are comfortable with order and control. I had to learn that once I left my office and cockpit, I had to switch from military officer to normal husband and dad. My family is not a military unit performing inspections and national security operations. They do not require training manuals and command and control procedures to live. They do require leadership and mentoring, but mostly my love and affection.

Looking back, I was right when I stated that $C = D$, because C *does equal D* in the sense that control leads to destruction. I was so serious about everything, until I almost lost what I valued most—my family. After coming to grips with my flaws and the impact of my actions, I changed my ways from a controlling person to a mellower guy who still gets results. It can be done, because I live my life that way now. I am still driven, with a strong passion for life and work and accomplishing my dreams. However, my expectation on how others should perform is altered. I accept people for who they are and not what I wish them to be. Instead, I focus on aspects of *my* life that I wish to improve. I see myself for who I really am.

My daughter's childish behavior that morning helped me realize that the fruit did not fall too far from the tree. I encouraged Gabriella to lighten up and not be so hard on herself. My efforts to motivate Gabriella to turn her frown upside-down helped me reflect on my own life. I now find myself enjoying life a lot more. All that stress before, and for what? Instead, I now look back and smile. You can too, as long as you remember one thing: C = D.

God help me not be so controlling. Send your angels to poke me in the ribs if I lose the big picture. Help me see myself as I truly am.

ARE YOU A CONTROL FREAK? Be honest. Do you like having everything in order all the time? What actions can you take to release the urge to control? What aspects of yourself do you purposefully overlook? What do you want to improve about yourself?

Resources

Located near Kansas City, Missouri, Diakonos Counseling (http://diakonoscounseling.com) believes in healing life's problems through integrating sound Christian principles for the mind, body, and spirit. For those not near Kansas City, Operation Military Family offers a couple's check-up, family assessments, and a battle-ready action plan. Learn more about these organizations in the Resources section in the back of this book.

TWENTY-SEVEN

Chicks' TDY

The Essence of Military Life

A friend loves at all times.

Proverbs 17:17

Teenage-like squeals and giggles ricocheted off the metal carousels, filling the once-quiet baggage claim with a New Year's Eve atmosphere, even though it was early March. As each military wife arrived from various statewide locations, the cheers multiplied. Camera flashes circled the room, and curious travelers rubbernecked to glimpse what recent celebrity graced the Nashville airport. Twenty years had passed since eleven of the original thirteen women stationed together at McConnell Air Force Base in Kansas were reunited. Now, the giddy forty- and fifty-somethings rejoined for a weekend of renewing friendships, reliving old memories, and creating wonderful new ones.

Denise, the group's social ringleader, masterminded the "Chicks' TDY" reunion after her husband left the Air Force to join the "real world's" workforce as a commercial pilot. Although Denise adjusted to civilian life as quickly as ants rebuild their home after a forced relocation, her patriotic heart remained with her military sisters. So every year she sends her gracious husband and kids to family and friends' homes. She then transforms her Southern home and lake cabin into guesthouses for military "chicks" to reunite the scattered "Stitch Club," a military wives group that met weekly for three years to work on creative projects.

My first encounter with the Stitch Club occurred exactly one day after my family moved to McConnell AFB. We bided our time in a base temporary living facility (TLF) until our base house was ready. I was on light bed rest with my second pregnancy after leaving Griffiss AFB in New York. Denise and Cynthia, two happy-go-lucky "Stitch" wives, dropped in to welcome me, introducing themselves as the Sunshine Committee. Their cheery demeanor and "welcome to our squadron" pies eliminated the "new-friend" anxiety that shadows military moves.

Three weeks later, my beautiful son Antonio bounced into the world. Stitch members I'd never met, or barely knew, gathered for a wonderful baby shower. Unknowingly, I entered a jam-packed room of soon-to-be-lifelong friends. Strangers throwing a baby shower with all the frills dumbfounded me. While I unwrapped handmade, satin-covered hangers, they invited me to join their Stitch Club. The answer no would have been as welcome to them as an IRS audit.

I soon discovered that weekly Stitch Club equaled group therapy minus the hefty price tag. This hodgepodge of military wives included personalities as opposite as Donald Trump and Mother Teresa, and we celebrated our differences. Stitch members toted needlepoint projects to sew, photos to put in scrapbooks, Christmas cards to address, magazines to browse through, etc. It didn't matter what the project was, Stitch Club allowed us to meet with fellow spouses and swap parenting victories, spouse challenges, and military life hardships.

When our husbands offered no sympathy regarding the perils of potty training, worries of a child readjusting to a new school, or the need to talk to someone without a milk moustache, Stitch Club filled the void. When one woman fell, the others picked her up, dusted her off, and injected shots of love to renew her spirit. We celebrated our children's birthdays and their first teeth. We organized midnight cookie drives[25] and filled our cupboards with newly purchased Tupperware and woven baskets in efforts to support our stay-at-home moms' business ventures. We donned our husband's flight suits, celebrating their military fraternity, and proudly waved to their planes flying overhead. Together we walked through the fires of marital challenges, the damage from disastrous tornados, and even the loss of precious life. Within those three years, several Stitch members experienced heartbreaking miscarriages. In addition to child care and delivered dinners, every Stitch friend was ready to give a needed hug for strength and be a strong shoulder to cry on when the waves of emotion flowed. Unfortunately, the losses didn't end there.

On September 19, 1997, our dear Stitch Club friend Cynthia was informed that her husband of eighteen years, Major Clay Culver, did not survive the B-1 bomber crash that occurred on a Montana

---

25. A cookie drive is an effort arranged by spouses to provide homemade cookies for military members working long shifts during a military exercise. A military bus drives around the flight line and drops off morale-boosting snacks to the troops.

prairie. Liz, another of our Stitch Club friends, who was stationed with Cynthia in South Dakota, upheld Cynthia when she had no strength to stand. Cynthia said, "Liz stayed over and slept beside me. To this day, that connection . . . so I didn't have to lie there alone, was one of the sweetest things ever. Just hearing someone breathe beside me helped me. I wasn't alone." For three years, our group not only cross-stitched needlepoint and glued photos into scrapbooks, but we also sewed together and cemented close friendships—life's experiences were the binding thread.

Eventually, military reassignments scattered our little group. Yearly Christmas cards sadly replaced our treasured weekly stitch time—until Denise converted weekly Stitch into annual Chicks' TDY reunions. After our initial meeting over twenty years ago, this gathering marked the first reunion that nearly all of us attended.

After the wave of hugs ebbed, our current of boisterous laughter traveled to the parking lot. We piled zebra-striped and ribbon-garnished luggage into two minivans to commence the weekend's events. While driving to Denise's cabin, we joked how conversation topics had evolved seemingly overnight from stretch mark cream and diaper prices to wrinkle removers and college tuition costs. Although bleacher sitting now felt more comfortable due to our bottoms' extra padding and our faces grew more attractive to draw for artists interested in facial shading, our friendship bonds remained untainted. This phenomenon amazed us.

Friends perfume our lives' flower gardens. Some friends are annuals; they fragrance our lives for a short time. Others are perennials; they celebrate the beautiful seasons of our lives and brave the harsh weather as well. True friends encourage us when the weight scale exposes the Dorito binges, and then they cheer the half-pound loss. They accept our shortcomings without waving the judgment flag. Friends transform into house cleaners, babysitters, and surrogate mothers when we become ill and our families live four hundred miles away.

Each assignment blessed me with wonderful, amazing women. I can't imagine TDYs and deployments without friends' support. However, many wives become isolated and depressed, and disengage from activities when relocating or when their husbands deploy. Numerous spouses enter "shutdown" mode after receiving relocation orders because leaving friends is so painful. While departing McConnell AFB and fighting back tears, I was offered wise words from Cindy, my neighbor and dear friend: "Remember, God knows the hearts that need touching. He has already chosen those friends for you at the next base."

Friends are lifelines in crisis, and they are beacons when we need guidance. Don't make the mistake of alienating yourself from military friends or potential friends. If representatives from the spouses' group neglect to welcome you to your new base, then call *them*. Accidental oversights do occur. Also, military bases provide numerous volunteer opportunities to serve the community and enjoy new people. Commanders' wives will happily connect you to them. Base hobby centers offer a variety of classes, and outdoor recreation centers coordinate activities frequently.

If you notice a friend becoming isolated, show your friendship through action. Engage him or her in activities. If you are concerned that your friend may have severe depression, direct him or her to your base chaplain, Military Family Resource Center, Department of Defense family life counselors, or militaryonesource.com. Depression paves the road for eating disorders, drug and alcohol abuse, and even suicide. In addition, marriages are increasingly becoming a casualty of combat–related depression.

When I recall the twelve geographic locations where I hung my hat over the years, memories of the base layouts fade, home facades mesh together, and differentiating one town's streets and stores from the others grows difficult. But when I think back to the friendships in each location, vivid faces materialize in my mind. I hear a friend's sweet laughter and encouraging words as if she sits across from me. I recall strolling through Italy's villages at Christmastime, painting "Special Day" ceramic plates in Alabama, and perusing handmade pottery in Poland because of the friends who made those times special. Each state or country's beauty and culture is significant, but the essence of military life is our friendships.

Lord, thank you for the seasonal friendships you have placed in my life as well as the permanent perennials. Let me be that friend that loves at all times. Nudge me when someone needs a kind word or a shoulder to lean on, and help me heed your call.

DO YOU HAVE A FRIENDSHIP NETWORK IN PLACE? How do you step out of your comfort zone to welcome a new spouse to your base? Are you engaged in activities that nurture ongoing friendships or do you need to become more involved to meet new friends?

TWENTY-EIGHT

How Ya Doin'?

The Importance of Listening

My dear brothers, take note of this: Everyone should be quick to listen, slow to speak . . .

James 1:19

"How ya doin'?" I asked an oncoming foreign exchange officer as I rushed to get to my first class at Air University. The packed halls reminded me of New York City's Grand Central Station, where everyone is too busy to even notice you. The officer, dressed in an elaborate dark blue non-American military uniform, abruptly stopped and extended his right hand. He said, "Hello, I am Peder from Sweden." Peder smiled as if he had just found a hundred-dollar bill. He continued, "I have a question, if you don't mind. Why do people greet me by saying, 'How ya doing?' When I stop to answer, they continue to walk by."

I grinned at his innocent question and explained that in America, we say "How ya doin'" without a question mark as a substitute for "Hello" or "Have a good day." He was grateful for my answer, and we struck up a conversation. Peder shared family challenges that he faced while transitioning to life in America, and he invited my family to his home for a traditional Swedish dinner.

When we arrived, his family met us at the door singing traditional Swedish songs, and then shared their unique Scandinavian cuisine. The pickled herring and smoked eel raised our eyebrows, but the experience was outstanding. I left Peder's home realizing that I would have missed this great friendship opportunity had I not taken the time to listen.

While stationed in Europe, I understood the importance of listening, only from a different point of view. As the new Master Air Attack Plan Chief, I reported to Spanish officer Colonel Javier Olmos as part of an international team of joint officers. Our mission was peacekeeping operations in the Balkans after Operation Allied Force. My family accompanied me to this remote assignment; however, my oldest son, Nico, attended high school in England at a Department of Defense boarding school. Children of military members and government officials who lived in non-English speaking locations or areas too dangerous for children to attend local schools were offered this specialized education.

On my first day of work, Colonel Olmos invited me to his office. During our meeting, I realized that I was doing most of the talking. He was quiet, allowing me to ramble on about our important mission and recommended strategies for success. However, Colonel

Olmos seemed more interested in getting to know the man "Tony" rather than the lieutenant colonel. He asked how my family was adapting with living in a foreign country.

During our conversation, I told him that Nico was living away from home. He leaned back and asked, "So how are you doing?" I sat there perplexed and responded, "Excuse me, sir? I am doing fine, thank you." He shook his head. "No, Tony, how are *you* doing? It must be difficult for your family to be separated." Deep emotions stirred within me. I love my son and sending him away was beyond tough. It was the first time Nico was away from home and it devastated me. The colonel could tell that he struck a nerve by my change in demeanor.

After the conversation, Colonel Olmos asked if I would attend a meeting in London on behalf of the organization. The meeting was being held near Nico's school. The colonel's care elevated my opinion of his leadership skills beyond the military ranks. Colonel Olmos taught me the importance of being a superior leader through listening.

As military servicemen, it is common for us to wear a macho warrior attitude. It requires skill and quality time for others to break through soldiers' facades. Through Colonel Olmos, I learned not only the importance of listening to coworkers, but the value of listening to my own family as well. During the week I wrote this chapter, I was put to the test.

I was home one morning because I was scheduled to fly a B-2 night mission, so I decided to drive my daughter, Gabriella, to school. During the car ride, she excitedly shared her plans for the day. My mind wandered to the upcoming flight and the many thunderstorms that I would encounter. A few minutes into the ride, she sternly asked, "Dad, are you even listening?" She was right. I was not. The words were going in my ears, but I didn't process them. Knowing that I hurt my little girl's feelings, I shut the radio off and zeroed in my attention on my little princess, who was visibly upset. I apologized, and then I listened to each word she said. When she asked a question, I restated in my own words what I thought she asked. She appreciated my sincere willingness to listen and I was off the hook.

As military personnel, without realizing it, we may come across as militaristic or forceful and blunt in our tone and speech, especially to loved ones and civilians (as my family often reminds me). After all, in our professions, we deal with concise forms of communication that demand precise understanding with little room for error. However, considering where I am and who I am communicating with now helps me determine *how* to communicate. I am more sensitive to family members and civilians who do not share the military workplace environment.

In addition to the tone of communication, I'm also learning the importance of slowing down and listening more effectively, rather than dominating a discussion. It takes effort to listen and think before talking. A good listener is attentive to nonverbal cues, tone of voice, and context. Being quiet challenges me, because my natural desire is to interact with others, but I am learning.

My dad taught me an Italian saying that rings true: "*Parla poco e senti assai*," which translates to, "Speak a little and listen a lot."

Relationships are essential in life, and effective listening is key to building strong bonds. By the simple act of listening, friendships are forged and relationships strengthened, and people feel valued and respected.

So, how ya doin' today?

Lord, teach me to be quiet and listen more effectively rather than talk without considering others. Open my ears and guide my tongue so I can be a more effective listener.

ARE YOU A GOOD LISTENER? Do you find yourself doing most of the talking during conversations with others? How can you train yourself to listen more effectively?

TWENTY-NINE

Sex and a Bag of Chips

Fulfilling Our Spouse's Love Language

The wife's body does not belong to her alone but also to her husband. In the same way, the husband's body does not belong to him alone but also to his wife. Do not deprive each other except by mutual consent and for a time, so that you may devote yourselves to prayer. Then come together again so that Satan will not tempt you because of your lack of self-control.

1 Corinthians 7:4–5

It was 9:00 a.m. when the phone rang. "Penny, is everything all right? I dropped by your house this morning, and the boys were watching TV while wolfing down a bag of potato chips. I asked where you were, and Nico said you were doing bills. I know you don't feed your kids chips for breakfast, so I just wanted to make sure everything was okay."

I assured Annette that I had not fallen and lost consciousness while my junk food–loving boys hurdled over my limp body to invade the off-limits snack cupboard (although the scenario was completely possible). I confided my challenge to have intimate husband/wife time. "Potato chip mornings" after breakfast, buddied up with an episode of *Rugrats*, allowed Tony and me to steal a half hour (if it wasn't a rerun) of alone time together while mommy and daddy "did bills." We never encourage lying, so the stack of statements accompanied us into the bedroom, and occasionally, we glanced at them.

I admit bribing my children with empty, greasy carbs is not the healthiest method to create couples time, and I'm sure parents have invented much more cunning rituals than mine; however, the fact is that couples require private time together to maintain a healthy marriage. For many women, shuffling intimacy with busy schedules and family responsibilities is challenging. Add TDYs and deployments to the normal military demands and spouses have better odds of finding a swan in a blizzard than finding alone time with their husbands. Regardless of busy lifestyles, it's crucial that couples make room at the crowded table in the restaurant of family demands for the special guest called intimacy.

Let's face it. Men and women's sexual needs differ. During intimate times, men have built-in earplugs that miraculously block out little Johnny's screams for help as big brother lassos him with the vacuum cord, wrestles him to the ground like a rodeo cowboy, ties his hands and feet together, and then force-feeds him leftover broccoli. A husband can even phase out his mother-in-law's five-minute phone message describing her bladder condition. Most women, on the other hand, have a built-in sonar device for their children's voices and can't ignore the "Can I get more chocolate milk" pleas and the "Johnny took my Legos!" accusations. Most women enjoy and prefer time alone with their spouses without distractions.

Men's sexual drives switch on as fast as a wireless Internet connection. Click. Libraries of information rapidly stare back from your screen within nanoseconds. Click. Every recipe known for cooking Texas chili appears lickety-split at your fingertips. Need to know how earwax forms or the wait time for the Space Mountain ride at Disney World? Hit search and eureka! A wife utters an innocently spoken word that can be *remotely* related to sex, and a stoic business executive instantly transforms into to a giggling teen with raging hormones. Click. Just the glimpse of a woman's bare shoulder or an exposed leg bombards a man with sexual thoughts. Click. If a wife describes detailed plans for intimate time that evening during breakfast, a man concentrates on work like a toddler facing a plate of brussels sprouts when a chocolate cake rests in the middle of the table.

Most women's sexual needs, on the other hand, sluggishly dial up like those clumsy old dinosaur PCs of the '90s. Switch it on. Make coffee and breakfast, and vacuum the house while you wait for it to boot up. Log on, and get the car's oil changed while waiting for connection. Similarly, most women's sexual desires "start up" gradually as well.

Women need jump-starts to rev their sexual motors. Men wouldn't dare start a lawnmower without priming the gas bulb first. Women need men's love "squishes" that prime her sexual desire as well. Kind words spoken in the morning, unexpected caresses, doing her least favorite chore, "just because" gifts, talking uninterrupted twenty minutes a day, or prearranging a dinner out (childcare included) sets the sexual mood for a woman more than "Hey baby, wanna get it on?" or new lingerie will ever achieve.

Men, on the other hand, also need love, but sometimes—and I've reworded this numerous times without the desired impact, so forgive my bluntness—they just need sex. Women fare much better when they set their own stewing desires on the back burner to meet their husband's stirring needs. It's a funny circle. Once a spouse focuses on the partner's needs, his or her own desires become fulfilled as well—and the circle continues.

During the annual Chicks' TDY reunion (chapter 27), I asked my military friends, who have remained married to their original honeys for over twenty years, how they created intimate time through the busy seasons of raising kids and demanding careers. They all agreed that to keep a marriage healthy, intimacy cannot be ignored or unhealthy behaviors such as pornography or infidelity may fill the void. Here are their wise and quite comical tips to create and "spice up" intimate husband/wife time:

- Escape two weekends each year alone. Invite parents to watch the kids (they will enjoy the bonding time) or exchange a weekend of kid swapping with a good friend.
- When company visits for extended time, investigate different rooms in your home. Closets not only store clothes, and showers offer a great sanctuary for alone time.
- Make quick lingerie out of a barbecue apron.

- If you live on or near a base installation, call your honey to see if he/she can break away for a special lunch treat.
- Realize that junk foods can be healthy in non-nutritional ways.
- Visit your car or vehicle in a locked garage to create spontaneous fun.
- Text a provocative message about the night's plans and watch your spouse arrive home early.
- Get rid of "granny panties" and replace them with sexy lingerie. Don't worry about weight. He won't.
- Know that cuddling is not a necessity in time crunches.
- Pack sexy underwear in his lunch box instead of cookies. He'll thank you for the dessert.

Since more than a hundred thousand men and women are currently deployed, how do couples maintain intimacy while separated? Intimacy and sex are not the same. Intimacy is the emotional connection between two people, while sex . . . well, if I need to explain, you need to read a different book! The following tips will help couples maintain long-distance intimacy and give deployed honeys something to look forward to after returning home.

- Burn a CD full of meaningful romantic songs that remind you of those significant moments in your relationship.
- Each week, memorize the same Bible verse. Knowing you both are praying the same verse bonds couples together.
- Send a coupon book good for an array of special "services" valid upon return.

- When sending e-mails or text, use code words or symbols to replace intimate words. Talking in code will safeguard your messages from prying eyes.
- Send a pillow with your photo embellished on it.
- Mail recorded tapes to each other. Hearing each other's voices eases loneliness.
- Send monthly milestone cards to ensure your honey that you are counting the days to be together again.
- Send each other your short- and long-term goals, reassuring you both of your future together.

The military presents unique challenges to keep marriages intact, especially during long deployments. But when each spouse focuses on the other's needs, even when separated, sexual temptations stay at bay. Potato chip mornings will happen—at all times of the day—and healthier marriages will result.

Lord, thank you for giving me a partner that I can express my love to in all ways. Help me to focus on my spouse's needs, and help us to carve out intimate time in our busy lives.

HOW DO YOU PRIORITIZE HUSBAND/WIFE TIME? What challenges do you face in finding alone time? What can you change to increase intimate time while together and prevent future sexual temptation when you are apart?

THIRTY

I Know a Pilot Who

Encouraging and Building Integrity

Therefore encourage one another and build each other up.
1 Thessalonians 5:11

Only twenty B-2 stealth bombers exist as of January 2011. Each is valued at two billion dollars, which is more than its weight in gold. The B-2 program started with twenty-one bombers; sadly, one was lost in 2008. When I first heard of the mishap, my immediate concern was for the pilots. Both pilots ejected seconds prior to the crash and survived. They stayed with the aircraft until one wingtip hit the ground!

Within twenty-four hours of the accident, the Air Force assembled a safety team to investigate the destruction of this national asset. The safety team determines the causes of plane mishaps and makes recommendations to the Department of Defense's leadership for preventing future accidents. The Air Force encourages open and honest communication during a safety investigation by offering "safety privilege" to personnel interviewed, similar to the privilege between a priest and a layperson. Safety is paramount, and airmen understand that the information shared during a safety investigation is used only to enhance future missions.

As Whiteman Air Force Base's chief of safety, I facilitated a pilots' meeting and offered "safety privilege" with the hope of improving flying operations. After dividing the room into groups of twelve, I encouraged team members to share safety-related experiences from their careers. I called the meeting "I know a pilot who." Each pilot began his or her story with the words "I know a pilot who . . ." and then the pilot would complete the sentence. Pilots could be talking about another pilot, but maybe not. My goal was to get stories flowing without fear of incrimination. Afterward, each group shared its best story. The result was amazing—everyone learned from each other's eye-opening accounts. By encouraging open communication, we were empowered with useful information that made us stronger.

I use the same concept of "safety privilege" with my family to encourage honest communication and build trust. My children know that if they tell the truth, no matter what, they get an automatic "get out of jail free card." There will be no punishment as long as the truth is told. A quote that I heard and use is "If you have an ugly baby, well then you have an ugly baby." Just fess up and move on. The Monetti truth policy is unwavering and lasting, meaning that confessions during "safety privilege" cannot be used against a child later. I asked Nico to recount a story on this subject:

> Once I went ding-dong ditching with Alex. Some
> lady saw us running away and called Mom to tell on

us. Mom was really upset at me, but you came into my room and asked what happened. I was nervous at first and thought about lying and saying I didn't do anything, but I decided to tell you the truth. To my surprise, you thought it was funny, bailed me out of trouble with Mom, and told me stories about how you and your friends used to do the same things. Only you'd wedge toothpicks in the doorbells so they kept ringing! I felt relieved that I'd been honest with you, escaped trouble, and bonded with you. I felt like you had my back even when I did crazy things and I appreciated that.

Afterward, I explained that we were both wrong in our actions, but I did not punish Nico because I value integrity.

Hearing the truth sometimes hurts, and bad actions have consequences, but I prefer to offer my family amnesty for the sake of integrity. By encouraging others to share what is on their mind, stronger relationships develop. Everyone makes mistakes, and it is easy to get angry when errors occur. There are legitimate reasons for getting upset. Even Jesus got angry when people used a holy place for greedy purposes (see John 2:13–17). However, righteous anger should be the exception rather than the rule. Effective communication requires patience and understanding. Encouraging and building up others takes effort. Destroying is easy. Let me illustrate this point.

Whenever my family goes to the beach, you will find Penny building sand castles. She is an amazing artist, and her sand art is crafted with precision. She has created seven-foot alligators, exotic birds, and sand castles with drawbridges, moats, and all. Her sand art takes hours to create, but only seconds to destroy. I have witnessed children running through her creations and within moments the beauty that was there has crumbled away. Similarly, building relationships and encouraging people requires concentrated effort, whereas tearing people down or constantly finding fault is reckless (and harmful). Destroying is easy. Building requires effort. Only you know what type of person you are—a builder or a destroyer.

Military men and women are structured, disciplined, and mission-oriented. We have a mission to do and sometimes forget that we deal with human beings and not robots. When others shirk responsibilities, some get angry. I have served under the command of so-called leaders that yell and practically rip people's heads off when their expectations are not met. These militant control-mongers are no leaders. They lack their men's respect. Their rank is valued, but that is about it. I have also been blessed with outstanding leaders who I would follow blindly into battle because I know they have "got my back." Again, destroying is easy but building requires effort.

A true leader is a *VIP*. He or she provides *Vision* and possesses the communication skills to motivate others. Leaders know what they want, and they are able to point the team in the direction needed to accomplish the mission. A leader sees the finish line as he or she approaches the starting block, while others see the arduous course. Leaders have *Integrity*. Their word is their bond, and their speech is consistent with their behavior and character. Their words match their actions. Without integrity, you have diminished loyalty. Leaders have *Passion*. They encourage, inspire, and build. Enthusiasm salts their life and flavors their character. Effective leaders correct deficiencies in private and praise in public. Passionate leaders use their enthusiasm to motivate others.

Strong leaders are VIPs. As military servicemen, we may fly billion-dollar planes or sail nuclear-powered aircraft carriers. We may command hundreds of pieces of artillery and armored equipment or navigate satellites in space. However, none of that equipment matters without the individuals who operate it. Relationships are what matter most. By encouraging others, we build stronger relationships and teams.

Heavenly Father, open my heart and ears as I listen for your voice and guidance. Make me an encourager and not a destroyer. Help me to be nonjudgmental and more inclined to understand and listen.

HOW DO YOU ENCOURAGE OPEN COMMUNICATION?

Recall a time when you spent time listening and encouraging a friend or loved one. How did you feel afterward? When was the last time someone encouraged you? How did that make you feel?

THIRTY-ONE

It's Not All about You

Why We Serve

If anyone wants to be first, he must be the very last, and the servant of all.

Mark 9:35

Why do American servicemen and women voluntarily serve in the military? What gives us the courage to potentially lay down our lives for our nation? After twenty-three years of service with our joint force, I know why. We serve because we believe that we are part of something bigger than ourselves. We sacrifice because we share an ideal of service over self and an unshakable belief in America and her values.

America stands for freedom, providing opportunities for people to live their dreams without the stranglehold of oppressive governments and tyrants. Our country's founding fathers risked their lives for this ideal and serve as an example to us. In our country's history, many have died to protect this ideal. The heroes who have given their lives, beginning with the Revolutionary War to the current struggle against terrorism, share the same conviction that we are willing to die for our country because our sacrifice is worth the price of freedom. If there is one thing I know after serving with American soldiers, airmen, and marines, it is that our character of service over self binds us together.

Generally, heroes are given special status in society. But in a specific case, a hero lived among us who was not lauded while he lived, yet he changed the world forever. I believe that the greatest hero of all time was revealed to me as a teenager while on the subway in Brooklyn, New York. This hero shares common attributes with many American servicemen past and present.

During my routine train ride to school, I met a man reading a worn paperback, while I was reading a new book on Napoleon. We struck up a conversation, and I excitedly explained the genius of Napoleon. It amazed me how one man could make such a powerful difference. I asked him who he thought the greatest leader of all time was. Without giving it much thought, he replied, "Jesus." I chuckled at his response. He sensed my amusement and said, "When Napoleon died it was over. But when Jesus died and *then* rose from the dead, it all began." He explained how Jesus set a new standard by turning the world upside down. Love over hate. Turn the other cheek. Heal the blind. Raise the dead. Care for the poor. How Jesus was the Son of God and how He humbled himself on the cross for all. This gentle man shared how he had been addicted to drugs until he found Jesus. With passion, he explained how Christianity began due to the actions and choices of just one man.

He gave me his worn-out paperback, the Bible, and encouraged me to find the joy he experienced. I read that Bible cover to cover, and in time my understanding grew. I realized that a real hero serves others over his own needs and does not look for fame. Honor and glory are earned through actions. Striving to be last, rather than first, takes conscious effort. My new hero, Jesus, humbled himself by washing others' feet, by constantly caring for others, and by making the ultimate sacrifice—His own life. Jesus came as a servant, rather than a ruler, as a man who entered the city of Jerusalem on the back of a donkey "to seek and to save what was lost" (Luke 19:10). What I discovered is that it is not all about me, it's about serving others and making a positive difference. Jesus was the role model I was after. He is the role model our world needs.

Service brings meaning to life. When I was a young airman, my ambition for making rank and advancing in power was distracting me from what mattered most in life. One day after flying a B-2 training mission, I returned home and lay down on my bed. In my soul, I felt a desire to give more of my life and talents. While praying, I asked God for direction on what I could do with my life to serve others and God. In my heart, I felt Him respond with the idea of starting a Big Brothers and Big Sisters agency. Penny and I had mentored a boy on my previous base. Although our intent was to help an at-risk child in need, our experience with mentoring also blessed us. We felt good that we were making a positive difference in someone's life.

The county where we were stationed did not have a youth mentoring agency. The following day, I called Penny, who was helping a friend on bed rest. She shared her previous night's dream that we would start a Big Brothers and Big Sisters agency. At that moment, my prayer to serve God was confirmed in my soul—and I believed that He was behind this idea.

How Big Brothers and Big Sisters of Johnson County came to fruition over the next year is truly a miracle. Everything, and I mean everything, just fell into place. The nonprofit agency did not benefit Penny or me financially, but the joy we received through the years of watching hundreds of needy children get matched with positive role models made us "zillionaires." Not only have needy children received love and commitment from caring individuals, but priceless, lifelong friendships were forged as well.

When asked to speak in front of civilian and military dignitaries recognizing our efforts, I prayed for guidance on what to say, and the words just flowed. Big Brothers and Big Sisters was not about me and my skills to motivate and organize. It was about the Lord working through our team. It was about a team united in the belief that caring and committed people can make a positive difference when they show up and help others. We are all richer in life for the experience. I concluded my speeches by saying "to God be the glory." Jesus was and is my role model, and I try to live my life in His service while professionally living my life in service to my nation. I understand the distinction and am respectful to both.

American troops serve our great nation with passion and commitment. Many are not Christian, but they share the same belief of service over self. For those of us who are Christians, our actions testify to our individual faith. It is through our deeds that we are known, not by what church we attend. We serve our local communities as coaches, teachers, and mentors. We serve defending America against all enemies and proudly do so without looking for honor or glory. We are fortunate to be a part of this team. We must continue holding the torch of freedom, for we are America's hope for a better tomorrow.

Help me remember, Lord, to be a servant of others over self. Protect me as I do my part in defending freedom and help me live a good, rich life full of meaning and significance.

WHY DO YOU SERVE? What have you done lately to put others first? Is your focus on a life of service to others or on meeting your own needs?

Resources

After Deployment

Afterdeployment.org. This site provides self-care solutions targeting post-traumatic stress, depression, and other behavioral health challenges commonly faced after a deployment. Leading behavioral health experts from the Department of Defense, Veterans Affairs, and numerous civilian agencies conduct research and determine the best practices for delivering online mental health resources to service members, their families, and veterans.

Alcoholics Anonymous

www.aa.org. Alcoholics Anonymous is an organization that helps men and women recover from alcoholism. As the website states, "The only requirement for membership is a desire to stop drinking."

American Academy of Pediatrics

www.aap.org/sections/uniformedservices/deployment/videos .html. The Army Pediatric community has been active in developing DVDs for elementary age children (*Mr. Po and Friends*) and teens (*Youth Coping with Military Deployment: Promoting Resilience in Your Family*). These materials are available for free download via the American Academy of Pediatrics website, "Support for Military Children and Adolescents."

Armed Forces Crossroads

afcrossroads.com/famseparation/main.cfm. This web page is dedicated to those military members and their families and friends who are separated due to deployments, remote assignments, extended TDYs, natural disasters, and professional military education requirements. The information and resources provided here can make the military separation a positive one for you and your family.

Bible Gateway

Biblegateway.org. *Bible Gateway* is a tool for reading and researching Scripture online—all in the language or translation of your choice! It provides advanced searching capabilities that allow readers to find and compare particular passages in Scripture based on key words, phrases, or Scripture reference.

Called to Serve Ministry

pennymonetti.com. Visit our multifaceted military support website and locate "Called to Serve Ministry," which includes Spouses' and Warriors' corners where you can share your stories to give and receive strength confidentially from others in similar situations. The website's "R & R Room" offers encouragement, hope, and support for warriors and spouses through inspirational stories and related Scripture. A key feature is that spouses and warriors experiencing similar situations can encourage and pray for one another, and find helpful links and additional resources. Limited scholarships for When War Comes Home retreats for women touched by combat-related stress are available through this site.

We wish to recognize the military support organizations most helpful to military warriors and their families. Each year we will choose one worthy organization to support from this book's proceeds based on the feedback you send us. Visit our website's "Contest Corner" for more details.

Resources

Christian Military Wives

Christianmilitarywives.com. This site is a multi-denominational, Bible-based ministry of Christian Military Fellowship and was established by a group of Bible-believing military wives committed to wholeheartedly serving Jesus Christ through assisting military wives and their families. The group proclaims liberty to the captives and freedom for the oppressed, while providing a place of encouragement, growth, acceptance, fellowship, support, prayer, and the like for fellow military sisters in Christ.

Combat Faith

Combatfaith.com. This is a Christian encouragement and education site for individuals who wish to strengthen their faith in God; for those with challenging and serious issues related to relationship struggles, substance abuse, and alcoholism; and also for veterans with PTSD from combat experiences.

Day of Discovery

www.dod.org/Products/The-War-Within--Finding-Hope-for-Post-Traumatic-Stress--Part-I__DOD2186.aspx. "The War Within: Finding Hope for Post-Traumatic Stress" is a four-part online video series that encourages veterans and their loved ones whose lives have been drastically changed by war.

Defense Centers of Excellence (DCoE)

dcoe.health.mil. DCoE assesses, validates, oversees, and facilitates prevention, resilience, identification, treatment, outreach, rehabilitation, and reintegration programs for psychological health and traumatic brain injury to ensure the Department of Defense meets the needs of the nation's military communities, warriors, and families.

The Department of Defense

The twenty-four-hour, toll-free hotline number is (866) 966-1020. Many of the websites listed in the Resources section were created by the Department of Defense to assist combat veterans and their families.

Diakonos Counseling

Diakonoscounseling.com. This organization believes in healing life's problems through integrating sound Christian principles for the mind, body, and spirit. They offer compassionate care in the Kansas City, Missouri, area for those struggling with painful emotions, distorted thinking, and troubling behavior, as well as those desiring personal growth and more satisfying relationships. Their therapists are comfortable to talk to and experienced at integrating clients' religious and spiritual beliefs with the therapy and healing process. Therapists are available to lead conferences and speak on topics of interest to churches, businesses, or organizations.

Every Man's Battle

Everymansbattle.com. *Every Man's Battle* is a website through New Life Ministries (NLM) that offers online support groups, workshops, and other resources to help win the war on sexual temptation one battle at a time. In response to the loneliness of the soldier who is away from home, NLM created the Every Soldier's Battle campaign, which provides military personnel, both home and abroad, with resources that will help soldiers who choose to maintain sexual integrity and sexual purity. Kits cost fifty dollars, of which thirty dollars is tax deductible. NLM's goal is to provide ten thousand soldiers with an Every Soldier's Battle kit.

Family of a Vet

Familyofavet.com. This site gives advice on how to cope, survive, and thrive the "aftershocks" of combat including PTSD and Traumatic

Brain Injury (TBI). This difficult subject matter is explained in easy layman's terms.

Hope for the Heroes

Hopefortheheroes.com. Home to *411God*. The Center for Bible Engagement, a Ministry of Back to the Bible, offers hope to combat warriors and PTSD sufferers by making it easy to communicate with and learn from others dealing with similar feelings and past experiences. The 411God Hope for the Heroes Project is free and uses mobile phones to deliver encouragement—straight from Scripture—into the hands of soldiers, when they need it most. Making best use of social networking tools like Facebook, Hope for the Heroes is helping returning warriors help themselves and reconnect with other people and with God.

International Critical Incident Stress Foundation (ICISF)

Icisf.org. ICISF is a nonprofit foundation dedicated to the prevention and mitigation of disabling stress. ICISF provides leadership, education, training, consultation, and support services in crisis intervention and disaster behavioral health services to the emergency response professions, other organizations, and communities worldwide.

Military.com

www.military.com/military-fitness. You can spend an entire day on this site surfing through the array of special fitness programs, diets, and tips to achieve optimum health. The site is geared to accommodate everyone from kids to Special Operation Forces.

The Military Family Network

Emilitary.org. This site is the military candy store for website links pertaining to every aspect of family life. They offer a great relocation guide for before, during, and after moves, for every branch of Armed Forces Service.

Military Homefront

Militaryhomefront.dod.mil. It's worth the trip to wind your way through this site. Click on "Troops and Families," "Deployment," and then "Deployment Connections." This site offers many resources that can help military members, spouses, and families cope with the challenges and thrive during deployment or reserve mobilization.

Military Ministry

www.militaryministry.org. It is said that there are "no atheists in fox-holes." This is certainly true. Whether in peace or in war, American troops need faith to anchor their souls. Military Ministry serves military members, veterans, and families through direct ministry and partnerships with chaplains, churches, and organizations. Military Ministry offers marriage seminars, chaplain retreats, online devotionals and a prayer page, rapid deployment kits, military support resources, and leadership training to equip churches to be "bridges to healing" for returning warriors, veterans, and their families.

Military OneSource

www.militaryonesource.com. 800-342-9647. A 24/7 resource for military members, spouses, and families that deals with education, reloca-tion, parenting, and stress—you name it. Available by phone or online, the free service is offered by the Department of Defense for active duty, guard, and reserve service members and their families. The service is completely private and confidential, with few exceptions. Military OneSource offers three kinds of short-term, non–medical counseling options to active-duty, guard, and reserve members and their families.

MilitaryOneSource, in conjunction with the Children's Television Network, developed several DVD resources to assist preschool children and adolescents cope with deployment-related stress. The *Sesame Street* video "Talk, Listen, Connect" covers deployments, homecomings, changes, and grief. Find it at www.sesameworkshop.org/initiatives/emotion/tlc.

Military SOS (Significant Other Support)

Militarysos.com. This is a support and information resource for military spouses and significant others of all Armed Force branches, around the world. The site addresses all aspects of the military life, from basic and boot camp to relocation and retirement.

Military Spouse

milspouse.com. This is a fantastic site that encompasses all service branches and aspects of military life. Forum topics span from emotional eating to the right amount to tip a commissary bagger. Here, military spouses share fears, gather information, and receive needed encouragement—confidentially.

National Center for PTSD

Ptsd.va.gov. The National Center for Post-Traumatic Stress Disorder, Department of Veteran's Affairs, addresses the needs of veterans with military-related PTSD. Click on "For Veterans and the General Public," and then "Return from War." The page that comes up, "Returning from the War Zone," addresses transitioning from the warfront to the home front, and identifies signs that you or your war buddies might need some outside assistance, and where to go for assistance.

National Suicide Prevention Lifeline

War experiences and reaction to combat stress can lead depressed people to think about hurting or even killing themselves. If you think you or your family member may be feeling suicidal, contact the National Suicide Prevention Lifeline at 800-273-TALK (8255) or visit www.suicide preventionlifeline.org.

Not Alone

Notalone.com. *Not Alone* is a resource center and meeting room where warriors and spouses can confidentially meet online with other veterans and families for counseling and to discuss PTSD and other related topics with fellow veterans and family members. *Operation Foxtrot Papa* (OFP) is a group that meets weekly online for spouses and significant others of warriors who have come home from deployment. *Trench Talk* is a place for military spouses, girlfriends, and significant others to meet online informally in a quiet, confidential setting to discuss common (and uncommon) problems. *Parent Group* is an online meeting room for parents and other family members that focuses on reestablishing healthy relationships with their returning warriors. The eClinic is an immediate help, 24/7 call line and online support center for warriors and family members. To contact the eClinic for help or to learn more about counseling programs, call (866) 781-8010. The service is confidential and free of charge.

Operation Homefront, Wounded Warrior Wives

operationhomefront.net/www. Through on-site support communities, and a virtual community that includes an online discussion forum, Wounded Warrior Wives provides female caregivers with opportunities to build relationships, access resources, and enjoy brief moments of rest and respite from their care-giving responsibilities.

Operation Military Family

Operationmilitaryfamily.com. This site helps military couples "battle ready" their relationships. It offers a couple's check-up, family assessments, and a battle-ready action plan.

Operation Purple Family Retreats

www.operationpurplecampinfo.com. Operation Purple Family Retreats are Easter Seal retreats designed to allow military families to reconnect after experiencing the stresses surrounding a deployment and reintegration.

Our Daily Bread

Odb.org. This organization's mission is to make life-changing wisdom of the Bible understandable and accessible to all. Military members and families can sign up for inspiring daily devotions that relate to everyday life, which are delivered daily via e-mail, podcasts, mobile phones, Facebook, or through booklets mailed the old-fashioned way.

Point Man International Ministries

www.pmim.org. This ministry's mission is to connect the hurting veteran, as well as their families and friends, to others who have already begun the transition home after war. The organization states, "With Jesus Christ as our focal point, it is our desire to provide spiritual and emotional healing."

Real Warriors

realwarriors.net. The Defense Centers of Excellence (DCoE) for Psychological Health and Traumatic Brain Injury's goal is to promote the processes of building resilience, facilitating recovery, and supporting reintegration of returning service members, veterans, and their families. The Real

Warriors Campaign combats the stigma associated with seeking psychological health care and treatment and encourages service members to increase their awareness and use of these resources.

Tragedy Assistance Program for Survivors (TAPS)

www.taps.org. TAPS is a 24/7 tragedy assistance resource for *anyone* who has suffered the loss of a military loved one, regardless of the relationship to the deceased or the circumstance of the death. Founded out of tragedy in 1994 (see chapter 14), TAPS has established itself as a frontline resource for the families and loved ones of our military men and women, providing comfort and care through comprehensive services and programs, including peer-based emotional support, case work assistance, crisis intervention, and grief and trauma resources.

Veterans Administration (VA)

Va.gov. The Department of Veterans Affairs is the most comprehensive veterans' assistance organization. The VA operates programs to benefit veterans and members of their families. Benefits include compensation payments for disabilities or death related to military service, pensions, education, and rehabilitation. The VA also guarantees home loans, provides burial services for veterans, and operates a medical care program that includes nursing homes, clinics, and medical centers.

Vietnam Veteran Wives

www.vietnamveteranwives.org. Vietnam Veteran Wives reaches out to veterans and their spouses and families. VVW was created by the wife and widow of a Vietnam veteran who saw a much needed area for improvement concerning subjects such as benefits for spouses and children, VA claims, PTSD issues, Dependency and Indemnity Compensation (DIC) claims, and benefits after service. VVW is available to all veterans' wives and contains real-life stories of pain and hope so spouses dealing with PTSD and secondary PTSD will realize they are not alone.

When War Comes Home Retreats

whenwarcomeshomeretreats.com. A weekend event offered to women touched by the lives and service of combat veterans of any conflict. Everything regarding PTSD is available at this conference, the most important being hope. Limited scholarships are available on their website. The conference is based on the book *When War Comes Home: Christ-Centered Healing for Wives of Combat* by Christopher B. Adsit, Rahnella Adsit, and Marshele Carter Waddell (BookSurge, 2008). This book offers comfort and practical help to the wives of combat veterans struggling with the hidden wounds of war, including PTSD. Insights from the medical and counseling community are wrapped in biblical principles and the shared experiences of other military wives.

Support for Parents of Deployed Family Members
Go Army Parents

Goarmyparents.com. This site started as a personal blog about a mother's journey through her son's service, and over time evolved into a site for military parents, family, and friends. The organization now has supportive forums for parents to share their thoughts, experiences, and questions about the US military. Articles and weekly chat sessions are also offered.

Marine Parents

www.marineparents.com. Created in response to parents' needs to find information and to connect and share with one another during deployments, this site offers free services, connections, and outreach projects to support marines and educate marine moms, dads, spouses, families, and friends. They have helped over fifty thousand marines, recruits, and family members during boot camp, training, active duty, and deployments.

The Moms of Military Prayer and Support Group (MOMS)

www.momsofmilitary.com. This group began in a kitchen when two military moms began praying about their sons over cups of coffee. Ten years later, the group is more active than ever. Mothers across America and around the globe unite their prayers for their children serving in the military. The group is not only open to mothers and wives of loved ones serving but to *all* women related to anyone serving in the military. They gather to pray through an extensive e-mail network and support the troops and military families with hugs and prayers.

Navy for Moms

www.navyformoms.com. This site was created for the mothers (and loved ones) of those who are currently serving or considering serving in the US Navy. The site gives members a place to discuss issues with others who share common concerns. Moms share with fellow moms their fears, dreams, and personal experiences. The ultimate goal is to provide an environment of understanding, comfort, and belonging to all involved.

Support for Veterans Transitioning into the Civilian Workforce
Armed Forces Support Foundation

Armedforcessupportfoundation.org. This organization empowers service members transitioning from the military back into the civilian world by the use of technology and people working together.

Easter Seals

www.easterseals.com. As the largest provider of disability-related services, Easter Seals offers military and veterans systems of care to augment current reintegration efforts, providing military members, veterans, and their families supportive services and workforce development opportunities. Additionally, Easter Seals has tailored their exceptional therapeutic recreation and camping services programs and facilities to accommodate veterans with disabilities and their families.

Hire Heroes USA

Hireheroesusa.org. Hire Heroes USA's mission is to offer transition assistance, job search assistance, and job placement services to those who have honorably served in the US military—and to their spouses—in order to reduce veteran unemployment. Hire Heroes USA prioritizes veterans statistically most likely to be unemployed: veterans of Operations Iraqi Freedom and Enduring Freedom, and veterans who are wounded or disabled.

Military Connection.com

www.militaryconnection.com. This site features the most up-to-date online directory of resources, information, and vital information on military education and benefits including the GI Bill, employment opportunities, the latest military job postings, pay charts, and salary calculators for ex-military, veterans, military spouses, and family.

Military.com

Military.com. This site boasts of the largest veteran's job board in the world, and offers resume building, job career fairs, networking with other veterans, and much more.

The Veterans Corporation

www.veteranscorp.org. This organization's mission is to create more prosperous communities and a stronger national economy by fostering entrepreneurship and business opportunities for veterans and service-disabled veterans.

Vetjobs.com

vetjobs.com. A partner of the VFW's Military Assistance Program (MAP), this organization provides a transitioning service member with relocation and employment assistance and is available to assist *all* members of the "United States military family." This includes officer and enlisted, active duty, transitioning military, reservists, veterans, retirees; of the Air Force, Army, Coast Guard, Marine Corps, Merchant Marine, National Guard, Navy, National Oceanic and Atmospheric Administration, and Public Health Service; along with spouses, widows, widowers, and dependents; and Department of Defense civilians.

Get Involved! Support America's Military and Their Families

Perhaps you've always wanted to support the military but didn't quite know how. Maybe you don't have the finances to donate money, but you have time, or perhaps you have funds to contribute, but not a free minute to spare. The following organizations offer an array of avenues to fit the most diverse interests so you can support the men and women who defend America's freedom with your special gifts.

Adopt-a-Chaplain

www.adopt-a-chaplain.org. A Christ-centered ministry, Adopt-a-Chaplain is the only national charity that exclusively serves deployed chaplains. Their goal is to provide prayer for the chaplains and to provide tangible support that will enable chaplains to more effectively minister to the soldiers they serve.

American Legion

www.legion.org. This patriotic veterans' organization is devoted to mutual helpfulness and is committed to mentoring and sponsoring youth programs in communities, advocating patriotism and honor, promoting a strong national security, and continued devotion to fellow service members and veterans. Heroes to Hometown and Homeless Veterans are just a few of the worthy programs offered for veterans, families, and youth.

Heroes to Hometown

This transition program establishes a support network and coordinates resources for those for severely injured service members returning home from Operation Enduring Freedom and Operation Iraqi Freedom.

Homeless Veterans

A little more than one-fifth of the adult homeless population is veterans, According to the Veterans Administration. The American Legion coordinates a Homeless Veterans Task Force among its departments to augment homeless service providers and fill in the gaps where no assistance programs are available.

Hugs 4 Smiles USA

www.hugs4smilesUSA.org. When you volunteer, Hugs 4 Smiles USA assigns you a deployed hero's family and/or the warrior. You then send the warrior two care packages—packaged hugs—each month. If the soldier's family has also been adopted, they receive one package each month.

Kids Thank a Veteran

www.kidsthankavet.com. This organization has one main purpose—to show the men and women who serve in the United States military that Americans care. Children, who simply say, "Thank you for serving," to any veteran, can register on this site. But there is much more. On this site you will find information about the United States military, our veterans, women in the military, the American flag, veteran's holidays, United States military academies and services, groups that help veterans, veteran memorials and cemeteries, teacher activities, patriotic songs and crafts, great books to read, and photos of our veterans.

Operation Homefront

www.operationhomefront.net. Operation Homefront provides direct services to alleviate a military family's or individual's emergency financial burden, as well as counseling and/or recovery support. Other emergency funding assistance, which an applicant receives within twenty-four to seventy-two hours, includes emergency food and home repairs, financial assistance, critical baby items, vehicle repairs and donations, furniture and household items. Operation Homefront Village also provides housing for disabled service members and their families.

Operation Soldier Assist

www.soldierassist.com. This organization creates public awareness of the needs of young military men and women and encourages public participation in their Adopt-a-Soldier program to help deployed personnel. Operation Soldier Assist purchases and ships items needed by our troops.

Operation Ward 57

www.operationward57.org. Operation Ward 57 serves America's wounded who served in Operation Enduring Freedom and Operation Iraqi Freedom, and those who care for them. Walter Reed Army Medical Center (WRAMC) in Washington, DC, is the first stop for many of America's returning wounded service members from Iraq and Afghanistan. Known as "the amputee ward," the orthopedic Ward 57 at WRAMC houses some of the most severely injured patients for weeks or even months. Each person who buys a T-shirt from the organization not only shows his or her support, but also directly contributes to items for the Ward, patients, family members, and staff.

The Patriotic Pillow Project

www.patrioticpillowproject.org. Because war has left many of our service men and women wounded, this organization collectively extends appreciation to military heroes for their service and sacrifices. They stitch prayers and care into each pillow that is created for each special honorable recipient. A thank-you note is included with the gift of comfort, so each brave, wounded warrior will know how very much they are cared about. These pillows are compact but powerful.

Pease Greeters

www.peasegreeters.org. Patriotic individuals from Portsmouth, New Hampshire, welcome troops passing through Pease Air Terminal on their way to or from areas of conflict. They assemble in an hour's notice. Some drive as much as a hundred miles to be there. These individuals are too old to fight but young enough to care. They show respect for the troops and for their service to our country. As of May 1, 2010, the Pease Greeters have welcomed 356 flights at all hours of the day and night.

Team Marine Parents

www.teammarineparents.com. Team Marine Parents is comprised of teams of individuals nationwide that participate in walks, runs, marathons, bicycling, triathlons, swimming, motorcycle runs, and other events nationwide. The goal of Team Marine Parents is to promote awareness for communities to support Marine troops through participation in and donations to troop support programs from MarineParents.com.

The Thank You Foundation

www.thethankyoufoundation.org. The Thank You Foundation was started with the belief that the words *thank you* could transcend political, religious, and ideological differences and could provide an opportunity for every citizen to express their appreciation for those who serve and have served our country. The foundation accomplishes its mission by offering programs and services for veterans, military personnel, and their families.

The Veterans of Foreign Warfare (VFW)

www.vfw.org. The VFW provides numerous services to military service members and their families. Below are just a few. The three main efforts of the VFW Military Services Department are the Military Assistance Program, Operation Uplink, and Unmet Needs.

The Military Assistance Program (MAP)

vfw.org/Assistance/National-Military-Services/. MAP is the outstretched hand between the VFW and active duty, guard, and reserve military units. MAP offers grants to VFW Posts that participate in military unit functions, such as sponsoring farewell and welcome home activities, family readiness group events, or other sponsorship ideas.

Operation Uplink

www.operationuplink.org. Their motto is: "Until they come home, we'll bring their voices home." As the largest organization of combat veterans, the VFW knows the importance of keeping military families in touch. This program for deployed service members provides free phone time to active-duty military personnel and hospitalized veterans.

Unmet Needs

Unmet Needs helps military service members' families meet unanticipated financial demands due to deployments or other military-related hardships that can't be remedied through existing means and provides deployed warriors with the security of knowing that their families have additional support at home. Donations help qualifying members from the Army, Navy, Air Force, Marines, and Coast Guard, as well as members of the Reserves and National Guard in the form of grants—not loans—so recipients don't need to repay them.

Warmth for Warriors

www.warmthforwarriors.com. Members of this organization provide active duty and retired veterans with handmade, warm, wool hats and other comfort items to honor and support them.

Warrior Weekend

www.warriorweekend.com. Warrior Weekend provides weekends of rest and relaxation for soldiers and marines who have been wounded in combat in Iraq or Afghanistan and who are undergoing recovery at Walter Reed Army Medical Center. This outreach focuses on small groups of eight to ten and allows participants to enjoy themselves at various destination cities.

Wounded Warrior Project

www.woundedwarriorproject.org. This organization's mission is to raise awareness and enlist the public's aid for the needs of severely injured service men and women, help severely injured service members aid and assist each other, and provide unique, direct programs and services to meet their needs.

Note to the Reader

The publisher invites you to share your response to the message of this book by writing Discovery House, P.O. Box 3566, Grand Rapids, MI 49501, U.S.A. For information about other Discovery House books, music, or DVDs, contact us at the same address or call 1-800-653-8333. Find us online at dhp.org or send e-mail to books@dhp.org.

About the Authors

Lieutenant Colonel Tony Monetti, Director of Operations of the 13th Bomb Squadron at Whiteman Air Force Base, Missouri, is an Air Force Academy graduate, a combat veteran Command Pilot of the B-52 and B-1 planes, and presently flies the B-2 stealth bomber. His honors include the Distinguished Flying Cross and the Defense Meritorious Service Medal. The Discovery Channel, CNN, and MSNBC news featured his adventurous career as well as two military books, *B-2 Spirit in Action* and *Boeing B-52: Stratofortress Units in Desert Storm*. Tony is a sought-out Air Force spokesperson who motivates groups and top corporate organizations worldwide. His articles have appeared in several military publications, such as, *Flying Safety*, NATO's *Polaris Quarterly*, and the *Combat Edge*. Tony was honored as Warrensburg, Missouri's "2010 Man of the Year" for his outstanding contributions to the community.

Penny Monetti is the author of *Choose to Dance: A Mother/Daughter Guide to Tackling Life's Tough Issues* and is a member of the Advanced Writer's and Speakers Association (AWSA), which is made up of over three hundred of the top Christian women communicators around the country. Penny is certified to counsel trauma and crisis victims—specifically combat veterans and military families dealing with PTSD—through the American Academy of Christian Counselors. Helping children and adults realize their unique value fuels Penny's energy as a motivational speaker, mentor, Bible study leader, nurse, counselor, educator, and mother of three.

Together, Tony and Penny founded Big Brothers Big Sisters (BBBS) of Johnson County, recognized as a national BBBS model for successful start-up mentoring organizations. Penny founded Connected Hearts, an agency that assists needy and homeless children uniquely identified by school coaches, faculty, and nurses within the school district. Tony founded and leads the Lions Lake Initiative, an organization working to preserve and restore the Warrensburg, Missouri, community lake. Tony and Penny also own a popular Italian restaurant named Monetti's, which they utilize regularly to show appreciation for Armed Forces warriors and military families.

Raising three beautiful children ranks their top achievement—still in progress.

As a passionate speaking duo, Penny and Tony are eager to circuit military installations and organizations globally to share their riveting, humorous, and tenderhearted stories of faith to encourage families to overcome the unique stressors that military life imposes. They would love to visit your organization or military installation to encourage warriors and military families. Contact them at pennymonetti.com for speaking availability.